STEP·BY·STEP
GRILLING
COOKBOOK

EDITED BY SUSAN TOMNAY

CRESCENT BOOKS
NEW YORK

C O N T E

Olive Soda Bread, page 103.

Barbecued Lobster Tails with Avocado Sauce, page 71.

Thai Chicken Thighs, page 48.

Orange and Ginger Glazed Ham, page 93.

Pork Sausage Burger with Mustard Cream, page 29.

The Publisher thanks the following for their assistance in the photography for this book: Antico's Fruit World; The Bay Tree; Barbara's Storehouse; Barbeques Galore; Corso de' Fiori; Doug Piper's Butchery; Home and Garden on the Mall; HAG Imports; Pacific East India Company; Primex Products Pty Ltd; Potters Agencies.

Corn on the Cob with Tomato Relish, page 83.

Mango Upside-down Cake, page 110.

Leg of Lamb with Vegetables, page 98.

Step-by-Step

When we test our recipes we rate them for ease of preparation.

A single symbol indicates a recipe that is simple and generally quick to make—perfect for beginners.

Two symbols indicate the need for just a little more care and a little more time.

Three symbols indicate special dishes that need more investment in time, care and patience—but the results are worth it.

Front cover: Tangy Beef Ribs, page 33.
Inside front cover: Chicken Breasts with Fruit Medley (top) and Tandoori Skewers, page 56.
Inside back cover: Leg of Lamb with Baked Vegetables, page 98.

Grilling Basics

Some barbecues can be as formal as a dinner party, others as relaxed as a picnic on the beach. Whatever the case, you will need to be prepared—choose the barbecue that suits you best, light the perfect fire and prepare the food to its maximum advantage.

Types of barbecues

Fuel-burning Barbecues

Fixed barbecue Some backyards contain some sort of fixture for barbecuing; they are relatively simple constructions, usually made from bricks or cement and featuring two grills—the bottom for building the fire, the top for cooking the food. These grills are not generally height-adjustable, so cooking can only be regulated by adjusting the fire, or moving the food away from or toward the fire. Being fixed these barbecues cannot, of course, be put out of high winds or moved to shelter in the event of rain. Despite this, fixed barbecues are easy to use and maintain, and quite often are large enough to serve big gatherings.

Kettle barbecue One of the most popular styles of portable barbecue, the kettle features a close-fitting lid and air vents at top and bottom which allow for greater versatility and accuracy in cooking. Kettle barbecues can function either as a traditional barbecue, as an oven or as a smoker (see box on page 7 for preparation techniques). Kettle barbecues only burn charcoal (wood is not recommended) and are relatively small. The standard diameter is 22 inches so if barbecuing for large groups more than one kettle is probably required.

Brazier This is the simplest style of fuel-burning barbecue, of which the small, cast-iron hibachi is probably best known. A brazier consists of a shallow fire-box for burning fuel with a grill on top. Some grills are height adjustable or can rotate. Braziers are best fitted with a heat-reflecting hood so that food will cook at an even temperature.

Gas or Electric Barbecues

Although often more expensive than fuel-burning barbecues, gas or electric barbecues are very simple to use. In most cases, the gas or electricity heats a tray of reusable volcanic rock. Hickory chips can be placed over the rock-bed to produce a smoky flavor in the food, if desired. Sizes of models vary, the largest being the wagon style, which usually features a workbench, reflecting hood and, often, a bottom shelf for storage. While the small portable gas models, which require only the connection of a propane tank, are very maneuverable, the electric models are, of course, confined to areas where there is electricity available. Most gas or electric barbecues have temperature controls and accuracy is their primary advantage. Both gas and electric models can be fitted with rotisseries for spit roasting.

The fire

Fuel

Although it is traditional, wood is not an ideal fuel for cooking. It can be difficult to light and burns with a flame. Charcoal is a much better choice. It will create a bed of glowing heat which is perfect for cooking.

A kettle barbecue, although compact, can prepare a variety of foods.

Charcoal does not smell, smoke or flare and it is readily available in supermarkets or hardware stores. Pile the charcoal into a pyramid in the center of the firebox. If using self-lighting charcoal, simply ignite with a match. If not using self-lighting charcoal, soak the charcoal with standard charcoal lighter fluid, allowing it to soak into the charcoal for about 1 minute before lighting. Never use gasoline or kerosene on a barbecue. Gasoline may explode and

A gas-fueled barbecue cart featuring hood and work areas.

kerosene adds an unpleasant taste to the food. As a general rule, you can determine the amount of charcoal briquettes needed by spreading them out into a single layer, extending a little beyond the food that is to be cooked. On windy days, you may find that you need to use a little more charcoal.

Preparation

Once lit, fires should be left to burn for about 40–50 minutes before cooking. Charcoal will become pale and develop a fine ash coating when it is ready to use. (Wood will have a low flame and have begun to char.) If preparing a kettle barbecue, leave the lid off while the fire is developing.

Build the fire in the middle of the grate, so that any cooked food can be moved to the edge of the grill and kept warm.

Temperature control

A fire's temperature can be lowered by damping down with a spray of water. (A trigger-style plastic spray bottle is ideal.) Damping also produces steam which puts moisture back in the food.

The best and safest way to increase the heat of a fire is to add more fuel and wait for the fire to develop. Do not fan a fire to increase its heat because this will only produce a flame. Whatever you do, never pour flammable liquids on a fire.

Coals ready for cooking: Briquettes have developed a fine ash coating.

Cooking techniques

Most recipes in this book call for food to be cooked over a direct flame. Recipes using indirect cooking are in Chapter 8 and only possible on kettle barbecues and gas grills with more than one heat source. (See box on page 7 for explanation.)

Direct Cooking

As with broiling or frying in the kitchen, the less turning or handling of the food the better. Once the fire is ready, lightly brush the grill or flat plate with oil. Place the food over the hottest part of the fire and sear quickly on both sides; this retains moisture. Once seared, move the food to a cooler part of the grill or griddle to cook for a few more minutes. Barbecuing is a fast-cooking process so even well-done food will not take very long. Techniques such as stir-frying are ideal for the barbecue griddle.

Test meat for doneness by firmly pressing it with tongs or the flat edge of a knife. Meat that is ready to serve should "give" slightly but not resist pressure too easily. At first, the degree of doneness may be difficult to judge, but try to resist cutting or stabbing the meat; this not only reduces its succulence, but releases juices which may cause the fire to flare. Pork and chicken should not be served rare; so if in any doubt as to doneness, remove to a separate plate and make a slight cut in the thickest part of the meat. If the juices do not run clear, return to the heat for further cooking. Test fish for doneness by gently flaking the flesh

Retain moistness in the meat by searing quickly and turning only once.

Test meat for "doneness" by pressing gently with tongs.

in the thickest part with a fork. Cooked flesh should be white and opaque, but still moist.

Smoking

Wood chips or chunks come from hickory, mesquite, apple or alder trees and are available from supermarkets, barbecue specialists and some hardware or variety stores. Their smoke provides an extra and unusual flavor to the food.

Smoking is best done on a covered barbecue (see box on page 7 for technique) but can also be done on an open fire. Soak wood chips or chunks before using and toss onto the hot coals during cooking. When the wood burns, damp down with a little water to create more smoke. Wood chips burn quickly so should be added towards the end of the cooking process. Wood chunks should last through the entire cooking process.

If glazing meat, such as ham, and smoking together, always glaze before adding wood chips or chunks. (Please note that some woods, such as pine, cedar or eucalyptus will produce acrid smoke and are therefore unsuitable for cooking. Use only wood that is sold specifically for smoking.)

A barbecue griddle can be used to stir-fry vegetables.

Fish is ready when the flesh has turned opaque and flakes easily.

Rare, Medium or Well-Done?

Not everybody likes their steak, beef or lamb cooked for the same length of time. Test for "doneness" by gently pressing the meat with tongs or a flat-bladed knife. If in doubt, remove it from the barbecue and make a small cut in the meat to check its color.

Here is a guide to how the five classic degrees of "doneness" should feel and look.

Medium-rare: Springy to touch, with moist, pale-red center.

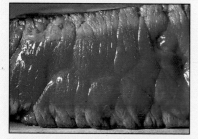

Very rare: Very soft to touch, red-raw inside, surface lightly cooked.

Medium: Firm to touch, pink in center and crisp, brown edges.

Rare: Soft to touch, red center, thin surface of cooked meat.

Well-done: Very firm to touch, brown outside and evenly cooked.

pastry bag and pipe individual servings over a piece of aluminum foil. Store, in refrigerator until required; place on food just before serving. Different flavored butters can also be served in their own individual dishes.

Always soften butter to room temperature before preparing.

Garlic and Cheese Butter

Beat 1/3 cup butter and 3 oz softened cream cheese until light and creamy. Add 1 crushed garlic clove and 1 tablespoon each chopped fresh basil and chopped fresh parsley. Beat until smooth. Using plastic wrap, form into a log shape and refrigerate.

Lime and Chili Butter

Beat 1/2 cup butter until light and creamy. Add 1 tablespoon lime juice, 1 teaspoon grated lime rind, 1 teaspoon chopped green chili and 2 teaspoons chopped fresh cilantro. Beat until smooth. Using plastic wrap, form into a log shape and refrigerate.

Savory Anchovy Butter

Combine 2/3 cup butter, 4 drained anchovy fillets, 2 chopped green onions, 1 garlic clove and 1 tablespoon grated lemon rind in food processor bowl. Process for 20–30 seconds or until mixture forms a smooth paste. Transfer butter to small serving dishes and refrigerate.

Pepper and Tomato Butter

Cut 1 large red pepper in half; remove seeds and membrane. Brush skin with oil. Place under preheated broiler for 5–10 minutes or until skin blackens. Put in brown paper bag for 5 minutes. Remove skin from pepper; discard. Chop flesh roughly. Combine pepper, 2/3 cup chopped butter, 4 drained sun-dried tomatoes in oil and salt and

Flavored Butters

These butters add the finishing touches to a meal and can be used instead of sauce. They are delicious on meats, fish and poultry as well as hot vegetables or spread over hot bread. Make 2 or 3 butters at a time and

store, covered, in the refrigerator for up to 2 weeks. Butters can also be frozen and stored for several months. Shape butters into a log and simply slice off the required quantity, then return it to the refrigerator.

Alternatively, place butter in a

Shape flavored butter into a log, freeze and slice rounds as required.

A pastry bag and a variety of nozzles can make interesting shapes.

Serving dishes can be stored in the refrigerator for several weeks.

pepper, to taste, in food processor bowl. Process 20–30 seconds or until smooth. Transfer to a serving bowl, cover in plastic wrap, and refrigerate.

Marinating and Basting

Because food is cooked quickly on the barbecue, some foods should be marinated beforehand. Marinate food, preferably overnight, but at least a few hours ahead in a non-metal dish, covered, in the refrigerator; turn meat in marinade occasionally. Vinegar, citrus juice or wine-based marinades break down and tenderize the fibers of the meat, and are ideal for tougher meats.

Oil-based marinades moisturize meats and are suitable for meat such as chicken or pork. Yogurt-based marinades are used with chicken or lamb, generally. The marinade will form a delicious crust over the meat when it is cooked. (See page 14 for marinade recipes.)

Drain food from marinade and cook food as quickly as possible. If marinade is oil- or vinegar-based, reserve and use to baste.

Basting While not all foods need to be marinated before being barbecued,

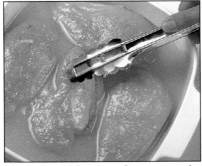
Meat should be turned once or twice during the marinating process.

most should be basted during cooking. Basting seals in moisture and prevents the food from sticking. Baste lightly on both sideswith olive oil or reserved marinade. A pastry brush, or clean, unused paintbrush is ideal for this. Do not use a brush with plastic bristles because the plastic may melt onto the food.

Planning your barbecue

Design your menu to take full advantage of the barbecue—remember, vegetables, kebabs, breads and even desserts can be cooked or warmed through easily.

Serve at least one salad with the cooked food. Salad dressings and special sauces can be made in advance and stored in a screw-top jar in the refrigerator. (See page 15 for salad dressing recipes.) Assemble salads up to a day in advance, but dress just before serving.

Light the fire about an hour before you are planning to use it and check the fire occasionally; it can easily go out if unattended.

Assemble all necessary utensils and accessories (for example, tongs, forks, knives, plates and basting brushes) before cooking.

Have plenty of snacks and drinks available for your guests, but place them well away from the fire.

Have a hose or water bottle standing by in case of emergencies. (As a general safety rule, do not attempt to barbecue in strong winds.) A flashlight may be useful if barbecuing at night.

Always extinguish a fire once you have finished cooking on it. If possible, clean out the barbecue as soon as it has cooled down by brushing or scraping the grills and racks. Discard any remaining ashes.

Indirect cooking

Indirect cooking roasts or bakes food more slowly than direct cooking. It also allows for adding fragrant wood chips to the coals which introduces extra flavor to the food.

To prepare a kettle barbecue for **indirect cooking:**

1. Remove lid; open bottom vent.
2. Position bottom rack in kettle. Heap coals and position some self-lighting charcoal or firestarters inside coals or soak charcoal with charcoal lighter.
3. Light fire and allow coals to develop to fine-ash stage. (Leave lid off while fire develops.) Place a drip-pan or baking dish on bottom rack. Position top rack; add food.

To prepare a kettle barbecue for **smoking:**

1. Prepare barbecue as above.
2. When coals reach fine-ash stage, add soaked wood chips; fill drip tray or baking dish with 4 cups hot water. Cover with lid until fragrant smoke develops.
3. Remove lid; center food on top rack. Cover with lid.

Position some self-lighting charcoal or firestarters within the coals.

Light fire and allow the coals to develop.

Place a drip pan underneath top rack when coals are ready.

Add wood chips or chunks to the hot coals.

NO-EFFORT EXTRAS

Hot Breads

GARLIC BREAD

Cut a French loaf into thick diagonal slices three-quarters of the way through. Combine 1/2 cup softened butter, 2–3 cloves crushed garlic, 1 tablespoon finely chopped parsley and pepper to taste in a small bowl. Beat until smooth. Spread mixture between each slice of bread. Wrap the bread in foil and place on baking sheet. Bake in moderate 350°F oven for 10–15 minutes or until the butter has melted and bread is hot. Alternatively, place the bread on a hot barbecue, turning occasionally to ensure even cooking.

BACON AND CHEESE BREAD

Combine 1/2 cup grated cheddar cheese, 2 tablespoons grated Parmesan cheese, 1 finely sliced green onion, 2 finely chopped bacon slices and pepper to taste in a small bowl. Across the top of an Italian loaf, at 3/4 inch intervals, cut diagonal slits 1/2 inch deep in one direction. Make similar slits in the opposite direction crossing over the first cuts, forming a diamond pattern. Place bread on a foil-lined baking sheet. Sprinkle cheese and bacon mixture over the top. Bake loaf in a preheated moderate 350°F oven 10–15 minutes or until cheese has melted and bacon is crisp. Cut into slices with a sharp serrated knife. Serve hot with butter.

TOMATO AND OLIVE BREAD

Cut a French baguette into 3/4 inch thick slices using a sharp serrated knife. Spread each slice with a small amount of green or black olive paste. Thinly slice 2 tomatoes. Place 1 or 2 slices of tomato on each slice of bread. Top with thinly sliced mozzarella or bocconcini (fresh mozzarella). Sprinkle with pepper and 2–3 tablespoons finely shredded basil leaves. Place on foil-lined baking sheet. Bake in preheated moderate 350°F oven 10–15 minutes or until cheese has melted and bread has heated through. Serve warm.

PESTO ROLLS

Combine 1/4 cup toasted pine nuts, 2–3 tablespoons freshly grated Parmesan cheese, 1–2 cloves peeled garlic, 2 tablespoons olive oil, 3 tablespoons butter, 3–4 teaspoons lemon juice, 1 cup fresh basil leaves and salt and pepper to taste in food processor bowl. Process 20–30 seconds or until smooth. (Add a little more butter or oil if pesto is dry.) Cut 6 small dinner rolls in half vertically. Spread each half with mixture. Toast rolls under preheated broiler 5–10 minutes or until heated through. Serve with shavings of Parmesan cheese. Alternatively, place roll halves together; wrap in foil. Place on hot barbecue, turning occasionally to ensure even cooking.

From top left: Bacon and Cheese Bread, Garlic Bread, Tomato and Olive Bread, Pesto Rolls.

9

CHICKEN AND CHEESE

HAM AND PINEAPPLE

SWEET CHILI VEGETABLE

MEXICAN

Dressed-up Potatoes

To cook potatoes: Wash and scrub the required amount of large baking potatoes; pat dry with paper towels. Prick potatoes all over with a fork or skewer. Wrap potatoes individually in aluminum foil. Place potatoes around hot coals of barbecue or on top grill of a preheated kettle barbecue. Cook potatoes 30–60 minutes (depending on potato size). Insert a sharp knife or skewer in the center to test if potato is cooked. (Flesh should be soft all the way through.) Remove foil from potatoes. Cut a large cross in the top of each. Squeeze to open; soften potato flesh by mashing gently with a fork. Mix a flavored butter (such as garlic butter—see recipe below) into potato flesh and top with topping of choice. Serve hot.

   Garlic Butter: (makes enough for 2 potatoes) Combine 3 tablespoons softened butter with 1–2 cloves crushed garlic. Mix well. Alternatively, add your favorite freshly chopped herbs or ground spices to butter to create your own flavored butter.

CHICKEN AND CHEESE

Mix a small amount of garlic butter into potato flesh. Top each potato with grated cheddar cheese, shredded barbecued chicken, coleslaw, salt and pepper. Spoon on a dollop of sour cream. Sprinkle with sweet paprika. Serve hot.

Serves 1–2

MEXICAN

Heat 1 tablespoon olive oil and 1 tablespoon butter in medium pan. Add 1 finely chopped onion, 2 teaspoons dried mixed herbs, 1 clove crushed garlic, 1 teaspoon each ground cumin and coriander. Cook 2 minutes or until onion is soft. Add 6 oz lean ground beef, 2 tablespoons tomato paste; cook 2–3 minutes. Stir in 1 chopped tomato, 1/4 cup canned red kidney beans, 1/4 cup bottled tomato pasta sauce; season with salt, pepper and chili powder to taste. Simmer 5–10 minutes to reduce liquid. Spoon over hot potato. Top with grated cheddar cheese, mashed avocado, sour cream and corn chips.

Serves 1–2

HAM AND PINEAPPLE

Heat 1 teaspoon olive oil in pan. Add 1 ham steak cut in small cubes. Cook 2 minutes. Stir in 2–3 drained chopped pineapple rings and 2 finely sliced green onions. Cook over medium heat 2 minutes or until heated through. Mix a small amount of garlic butter into potato flesh. Top with ham mixture. Sprinkle with pepper. Serve hot.

Serves 1–2

HERBED SOUR CREAM

CHICKEN CURRY

BOLOGNESE

MUSHROOM AND BACON

HERBED SOUR CREAM

Combine 1 cup sour cream, 1 tablespoon each of chopped chives, oregano and parsley, 2 teaspoons chopped mint, salt and pepper, to taste. Add 1 clove crushed garlic, if desired. Mix well. Spoon over hot potato.   Serves 2–4

SWEET CHILI VEGETABLE

Heat 1 tablespoon sesame oil in wok. Add 1 clove crushed garlic, 1 tablespoon soy sauce, 2–3 teaspoons sweet Thai chili sauce, 1 tablespoon plum sauce, 1 small thinly sliced carrot, 1/2 red pepper thinly sliced, 1/4 cup small broccoli florets, 1 small thinly sliced zucchini. Cook over medium heat 2–3 minutes. Add 2 sliced green onions; cook 1 minute more. Season with pepper and salt. Mix a small amount of garlic butter into potato flesh. Top with the vegetables. Serve hot.   Serves 1–2

BOLOGNESE

Heat 1 tablespoon oil in medium pan. Add 1 finely chopped onion, 1 teaspoon dried Italian mixed herbs and 1 clove crushed garlic; cook 1 minute. Add 8 oz lean ground beef. Cook 3–4 minutes until browned. Add 1/2 cup bottled tomato pasta sauce, 2 tablespoons tomato paste and 2–3 teaspoons balsamic vinegar. Cook, simmering, 3–4 minutes or until liquid has reduced. Stir in 1 tablespoon chopped fresh basil. Mix a small amount of garlic butter into potato flesh. Top with Bolognese and sprinkle with grated cheese. Serve immediately.   Serves 1–2

CHICKEN CURRY

Heat 1 tablespoon oil and 1 tablespoon butter in medium pan. Add 1 chopped onion, 1 clove crushed garlic, 2–3 teaspoons curry powder; cook 1 minute. Add 1 cup shredded barbecued chicken, 1 tablespoon golden raisins and 1 small peeled, chopped Granny Smith apple. Cook, stirring 2 minutes. Stir in 2 teaspoons flour. Gradually add 1/4 cup chicken stock and 2–3 tablespoons coconut milk. Stir until mixture boils and thickens. Season with salt and pepper. Spoon over potato, sprinkle with cilantro leaves. Serve hot.   Serves 1–2

MUSHROOM AND BACON

Heat 2 tablespoons butter in frying pan. Add 1 clove crushed garlic, 2 bacon slices julienned. Cook 1 minute. Stir in 10 large sliced mushrooms. Cook 3–4 minutes until soft. Stir in 1/4 cup heavy cream and 1 tablespoon chopped chives. Season with salt and pepper. Cook 1 minute. Mix garlic butter into potato, if desired. Spoon mixture over potato. Serve sprinkled with shavings of Parmesan cheese.   Serves 1–2

Sauces

HORSERADISH CREAM

Using an electric beater, beat 4 oz cream cheese until soft and creamy. Add 1 tablespoon each of mayonnaise and sour cream, 1–2 teaspoons minced horseradish or prepared horseradish and 1 tablespoon chopped chives, lemon thyme or parsley. Beat until combined. Serve with fish or beef.

CHILI BARBECUE SAUCE

Heat 1 tablespoon butter in small pan. Add 1 teaspoon ground cumin, 1/2 teaspoon each of ground coriander and paprika. Cook 30 seconds. Stir in 1 tablespoon sweet chili sauce, 1/3 cup bottled barbecue sauce and 2 teaspoons Worcestershire sauce. Mix well. Serve with lamb or beef.

TARTAR SAUCE

Combine 1/2 cup mayonnaise, 1 tablespoon sour cream, 1–2 tablespoons halved capers and 1 tablespoon finely chopped sweet pickles. Add 1 tablespoon chopped fresh dill, if desired. Serve with seafood or fish.

CREAMY MUSTARD SAUCE

Combine 2 tablespoons mayonnaise, 1/3 cup sour cream, 2–3 tablespoons Dijon or wholegrain mustard. Season with salt and pepper to taste. Mix well. (Add 1 tablespoon of your favorite chopped fresh herbs, if desired.) If sauce is too thick, add a little heavy cream to achieve desired consistency. Serve with beef or chicken.

TARTAR SAUCE

HORSERADISH CREAM

CHILI BARBECUE SAUCE

CREAMY MUSTARD SAUCE

CILANTRO MAYONNAISE

TOMATO SAUCE

GARLIC HERB HOLLANDAISE

TOMATO SAUCE

Heat 1 tablespoon olive oil and 1 tablespoon butter in small pan. Add 1 small finely chopped onion, 1 clove crushed garlic and 1–2 teaspoons Italian dried mixed herbs. Cook 2–3 minutes or until onion is soft. Stir in 2 large chopped ripe tomatoes, 1/2 cup tomato purée and 2 teaspoons balsamic vinegar. Cook 3–4 minutes. Remove from heat. Process until smooth. Season with salt and pepper. Serve warm or cold with burgers, sausages, steak or fish.

GARLIC HERB HOLLANDAISE

Place 2 egg yolks or 1/4 cup egg substitute in food processor bowl or blender. With motor constantly running, add 2/3 cup melted butter in thin stream. Process until thick and creamy. Add 2–3 tablespoons lemon juice or white wine vinegar, 1 tablespoon each of chopped chives, basil, oregano and 1 clove crushed garlic. Season with salt and pepper. Process 10 seconds to combine. Serve with fish, seafood, chicken or beef.

CILANTRO MAYONNAISE

Place 3 egg yolks or 1/3 cup egg substitute in food processor bowl or blender. With motor constantly running, add 3/4 cup light olive oil in thin stream. Process until thick and creamy. Add 2 tablespoons lemon juice and 1–2 tablespoons chopped cilantro. Process until combined. Season with salt and pepper. Vary the taste with herbs or garlic.

Marinades

LEMON AND WINE MARINADE

Combine 2 tablespoons lemon juice, 2 teaspoons grated lemon rind, 1 clove crushed garlic, 1 green onion, sliced, 1/4 cup white wine, 1/4 cup olive oil, 2 tablespoons brown sugar, 1 tablespoon each of chopped rosemary and lemon thyme. Mix well. Marinate lamb or chicken several hours or overnight in refrigerator, turning occasionally; keep covered.

LEMON AND WINE

TERIYAKI MARINADE

Combine 1/4 cup soy sauce, 2 table-spoons teriyaki sauce, 1 tablespoon grated fresh ginger, 1–2 cloves crushed garlic, 2 tablespoons brown sugar, 1/4 cup chicken or beef stock and 2–3 tablespoons sherry. Mix well. Marinate beef, pork or chicken for several hours or overnight in refrigerator. Turn meat occasionally; keep covered.

TERIYAKI

SPICED YOGURT MARINADE

Combine 1 cup plain yogurt, 1 finely chopped onion, 3/4 teaspoon each of ground coriander, cumin, garam masala and cinnamon, 1 clove crushed garlic, 1/2 teaspoon ground ginger, 1 teaspoon sugar, salt and pepper to taste and a pinch of cardamom. Mix well. Marinate lamb or beef several hours or overnight in the refrigerator. Turn the meat occasionally; keep covered.

SPICED YOGURT

APRICOT AND ONION MARINADE

Combine 1/3 cup apricot nectar, 1 teaspoon Worcestershire sauce, 1 tablespoon each of oil and balsamic vinegar, 1–2 tablespoons French onion soup mix, 1/2 teaspoon dried mixed herbs and 2–3 finely sliced green onions. Mix well. Marinate pork or chicken several hours or overnight in refrigerator. Turn meat occasionally; keep covered. (Add 1/4 cup red or white wine and a pinch of lemon thyme if desired.)

APRICOT AND ONION

MUSTARD AND HERB MARINADE

Combine 1/4 cup olive oil, 2 tablespoons balsamic vinegar, 2 teaspoons brown sugar, 2–3 teaspoons Dijon, German or wholegrain mustard, 1–2 teaspoons mixed dried herbs, 1 tablespoon chopped fresh parsley, salt and pepper. Mix well. Marinate beef or lamb several hours or overnight in refrigerator. Turn meat occasionally; keep covered.

MUSTARD AND HERB

Dressings

HONEY GARLIC DRESSING

Combine 1/4 cup peanut oil, 2 tablespoons lemon or lime juice, 1 teaspoon grated lemon rind, 2 tablespoons honey, 1–2 cloves crushed garlic, 1 tablespoon chopped fresh chives and salt and pepper to taste in screwtop jar. Shake until well combined. Pour over tossed green salad.

ORANGE AND SESAME DRESSING

Combine 1 tablespoon sesame oil, 2 tablespoons orange juice, 2 teaspoons toasted sesame seeds, 1 teaspoon grated orange rind, 1–2 teaspoons soy sauce, 3/4 teaspoon grated ginger and salt and pepper to taste in a screw-top jar. Shake until well combined. Pour over arugula and watercress salad.

CREAMY DRESSING

Place 2 tablespoons olive oil, 1 tablespoon mayonnaise, 1 tablespoon sour cream, 2 tablespoons lemon juice, 1 teaspoon brown sugar and salt and cracked black pepper to taste, in a screwtop jar. Shake until well combined. Pour over romaine lettuce. (Add 1 clove crushed garlic and 1 tablespoon chopped fresh chives to dressing, if desired.)

BASIL DRESSING

Combine 1/3 cup basil leaves, 3/4 teaspoon sugar, 1 clove garlic, 1/4 cup olive or vegetable oil, 1 tablespoon white wine vinegar, 1 tablespoon grated Parmesan cheese, 1/4 cup toasted pine nuts and pepper and salt to taste in food processor bowl. Process until smooth. Add a little extra oil to thin, if necessary. Pour over tomato salad.

VINAIGRETTE DRESSING

Combine 1/4 cup each of white wine vinegar and oil in a screwtop jar; season with salt and pepper, to taste. Shake until well combined. Pour over fresh garden salad. (Add 1–2 tablespoons of your favorite chopped fresh herbs to this dressing, if desired.)

**HONEY GARLIC
DRESSING**

CREAMY DRESSING

**ORANGE AND
SESAME**

BASIL DRESSING

**VINAIGRETTE
DRESSING**

BURGERS & SAUSAGES

BEST-EVER BURGER WITH HOMEMADE BARBECUE SAUCE

Preparation time: 20 minutes
+ 30 minutes refrigeration
Total cooking time: 25 minutes
Serves 6

1½ lb lean ground beef
8 oz lean ground sausage
1 small onion, finely chopped
1 tablespoon Worcestershire
   sauce
2 tablespoons tomato sauce
1 cup fresh bread crumbs
1 egg, lightly beaten
2 large onions, very thinly sliced
   in rings
6 wholewheat rolls
6 small lettuce leaves
1 large tomato, sliced

Homemade Barbecue Sauce
2 teaspoons oil
1 small onion, finely chopped
1 tablespoon balsamic
   vinegar
1 tablespoon brown sugar
⅓ cup tomato sauce
2 teaspoons Worcestershire
   sauce
2 teaspoons soy sauce

➤ PLACE GROUND BEEF and sausage in a large bowl.
1 Add onion, sauces, bread crumbs and egg. Using hands, mix until thoroughly combined. Divide mixture into 6 equal portions and shape into ⅝ inch thick patties. Refrigerate patties at least 30 minutes. Prepare and heat barbecue.
2 Place patties on hot, lightly oiled barbecue rack or griddle. Barbecue over hottest part of fire 8 minutes each side, turning once. While patties are cooking, cook onions in a skillet in a small amount of butter until golden.
To assemble burgers: Split rolls in half. Place bottom half on individual serving plates. Top each bottom half with lettuce leaf, patty, tomato slice and cooked onions. Top with a generous quantity of Homemade Barbecue Sauce. Cover with remaining bun half.
3 To make **Homemade Barbecue Sauce:** Heat oil in a small pan. Cook onion 5 minutes or until soft. Add vinegar, sugar and sauces; stir to combine and bring to boil. Reduce heat and simmer 3 minutes. Cool.

COOK'S FILE

Storage time: Burgers can be prepared up to 4 hours in advance and stored, covered, in refrigerator. Sauce can be made up to 1 week in advance. Store in refrigerator.

1

2

3

CHICKEN BURGER WITH TANGY GARLIC MAYONNAISE

Preparation time: 20 minutes
    + 3 hours marinating
Total cooking time: 15 minutes
Serves 4

4 chicken breast fillets
1/2 cup lime juice
1 tablespoon sweet chili sauce
4 bacon slices
4 hamburger buns
4 lettuce leaves
1 large tomato, sliced

Garlic Mayonnaise
2 egg yolks or 1/4 cup egg
    substitute
2 cloves garlic, crushed
1 tablespoon Dijon mustard
1 tablespoon lemon juice
1/2 cup olive oil

➤PLACE CHICKEN in a shallow non-metal dish; prick chicken breasts with a skewer several times.

1 Combine the lime juice and chili sauce in a cup. Pour over chicken; cover. Marinate several hours or overnight. Prepare and light barbecue 1 hour before cooking. Cut bacon in half crosswise.

2 Place chicken and bacon on hot, lightly greased barbecue grill or griddle. Cook bacon 5 minutes until crisp. Cook chicken another 5–10 minutes until browned and cooked through, turning once. Cut hamburger buns in half and toast each side until lightly browned. Top bases with lettuce, tomato, chicken and bacon. Top with Garlic Mayonnaise; finish with remaining bun top.

3 To make Garlic Mayonnaise: Place egg yolks or egg substitute, garlic,

mustard and lemon juice in food processor bowl or blender. Process until smooth. With motor running, add the oil in a thin, steady stream. Process until mayonnaise reaches a thick consistency. Refrigerate, covered, until required.

C O O K ' S   F I L E

Storage time: Chicken can be marinated 1 day in advance. Store mayonnaise up to 1 month in refrigerator.
Variation: For a tangy mayonnaise substitute lime juice for lemon juice and omit garlic.

1

2

3

MUSTARD BURGER WITH TOMATO AND ONION SALAD

Preparation time: 20 minutes
Total cooking time: 10 minutes
Makes 8 patties

2 lb lean ground beef
1/4 cup seeded mustard
2 teaspoons Dijon mustard
1 teaspoon beef bouillon powder
1 cup stale bread crumbs
1 egg
1 teaspoon black pepper
1/4 cup chopped red pepper

Tomato and Onion Salad
1 small red onion
4 tomatoes
2 tablespoons red wine vinegar
1 1/2 teaspoons sugar
2 teaspoons lemon juice

➤ PREPARE AND HEAT barbecue. Place ground beef in large bowl.
1 Add mustards, bouillon powder, bread crumbs, egg, black pepper and red pepper; mix well with hands. Divide mixture into 8 portions.
2 Shape portions into round patties. Cook on hot, lightly greased barbecue grill or griddle 2–3 minutes each side, turning once. Serve with Tomato and Onion Salad and bread of choice.
3 To make Tomato and Onion Salad: Chop onion and tomatoes into small cubes. Combine in bowl with vinegar, sugar and juice; mix well.

COOK'S FILE

Storage time: Patties can be prepared 1 day in advance. Store, covered, in refrigerator; barbecue just before serving. Salad can be made 1 day in advance. Store, covered, in refrigerator.
Hint: Substitute any mustard for Dijon mustard. German or American mustard will make a mild-tasting burger. English mustard makes a strong-tasting, hot burger.

1

2

3

APRICOT GLAZED SAUSAGES AND ONIONS

Preparation time: 20 minutes
Total cooking time: 15–20 minutes
Serves 4–6

3 onions
8 thick beef sausage links
1 teaspoon seeded mustard
1 cup dried apricot halves
3/4 cup apricot nectar

➤ PREPARE AND HEAT barbecue.
1 Cut onions in half; slice thinly. Cook onions on lightly greased barbecue griddle 5 minutes or until soft. Transfer to a plate; keep warm. Place sausages on barbecue griddle and cook 5 minutes or until well browned, turning frequently.
2 Slice sausages lengthwise, three-quarters of the way through. Cook, cut-side down, 5 minutes more or until browned. Add mustard, apricots and onions to sausages; stir.

3 Add nectar to sausage, apricot and onion mixture, a little at a time. Stir until nectar coats the sausages and begins to thicken. Repeat this process until all nectar is used. Serve sausages cut-side up, topped with onion and apricot mixture.

COOK'S FILE

Storage time: This recipe is best made just before serving.
Note: A barbecue griddle is essential to this recipe.

1

2

3

HERB BURGER

Preparation time: 20 minutes
Total cooking time: 15–20 minutes
Makes 8 burgers

1½ lb lean ground beef or lamb
2 tablespoons chopped fresh
   basil
1 tablespoon chopped fresh
   chives
1 tablespoon chopped fresh
   rosemary
1 tablespoon chopped fresh
   thyme
2 tablespoons lemon juice
1 cup stale bread crumbs
1 egg
pinch salt
pinch pepper
2 long French baguettes
lettuce leaves
2 tomatoes, sliced
bottled tomato sauce

➤ PREPARE AND HEAT barbecue.
Place ground beef in bowl.
1 Combine with herbs, juice, bread
crumbs, egg, salt and pepper. Mix
with hands until well combined.
Divide mixture into 8 portions.
2 Shape portions into thick rectangu-
lar patties about 6 inches long. Place
on hot barbecue griddle or grill. Cook
5–10 minutes each side until well
browned and just cooked through.
3 Cut each baguette into 4. Cut
each piece in half, horizontally. Top
bottom halves with lettuce, tomato,
herb burger and tomato sauce and
top bread halves. Serve immediately.

COOK'S FILE

Storage time: Meat mixture can be
made 1 day in advance and stored in
the refrigerator.

1

2

3

LENTIL AND CHICKPEA BURGER WITH CILANTRO GARLIC CREAM

Preparation time: 30 minutes
Total cooking time: 20 minutes
Makes 10 burgers

1 cup red lentils
1 tablespoon oil
2 onions, sliced
1 tablespoon curry powder
15 oz can chickpeas (garbanzo
    beans), drained
1 tablespoon grated fresh ginger
1 egg
1/4 cup chopped fresh parsley
2 tablespoons chopped fresh
    cilantro
2 1/4 cups stale bread crumbs
flour, for dusting

Cilantro Garlic Cream
1/2 cup sour cream
1/2 cup heavy cream
1 clove garlic, crushed
2 tablespoons chopped fresh
    cilantro
2 tablespoons chopped fresh
    parsley

➤ PREPARE AND HEAT barbecue. Bring large pan of water to boil.
1 Add lentils and simmer, uncovered, 8 minutes or until tender. Drain well. Heat oil in pan, cook onions until soft. Add curry powder; stir until fragrant; cool mixture slightly.
2 Place chickpeas, half the lentils, ginger, egg and onion mixture in food processor bowl. Process 20 seconds or until smooth. Transfer to a bowl. Stir in remaining lentils, parsley, cilantro and bread crumbs; combine well. Divide mixture into 10 portions.
3 Shape portions into round patties.

(If mixture is too soft, refrigerate 15 minutes or until firm.) Toss patties in flour. Shake off excess. Place patties on hot, lightly greased barbecue grill or griddle. Cook 3–4 minutes each side or until browned, turning once. Serve with Cilantro Garlic Cream.
To make Cilantro Garlic Cream: Combine the sour cream, heavy cream, garlic and herbs in bowl and mix well.

COOK'S FILE

Storage time: Patties can be prepared up to 2 days in advance and stored, covered, in refrigerator. Cream can be made up to 3 days in advance. Store, covered, in refrigerator.
Note: This recipe can be served as a vegetarian dish on its own, or as an accompaniment to other meat dishes. The Cilantro Garlic Cream is delicious with chicken or fish burgers.

1

2

3

HONEY SOY SAUSAGES

Preparation time: 15 minutes
  + overnight marinating
Total cooking time: 5–6 minutes
Serves 4–6

**8–10 thick beef or pork sausage
  links
1¼ inch piece fresh ginger
⅓ cup honey
⅓ cup soy sauce
1 clove garlic, crushed
1 tablespoon sherry
2 sprigs fresh thyme**

➤ PLACE SAUSAGES in a large
bowl or shallow non-metal dish.
1 Peel ginger and grate finely; combine with honey, soy sauce, garlic,
sherry and thyme; mix well.
2 Pour marinade over sausages.
Cover and refrigerate overnight to
allow flavors to be absorbed.
3 Prepare and heat the barbecue
1 hour before cooking. Lightly grease
barbecue grill or griddle. Cook
sausages for 5–6 minutes, away from
the hottest part of the fire, brushing
occasionally with marinade. Turn the
sausages frequently to prevent
the marinade from burning.
(Marinade should form a thick, slightly sticky glaze on the sausages.) Serve
with barbecued pineapple slices,
if desired.

COOK'S FILE

Storage time: Sausages can be
marinated up to 2 days in advance.
Store in refrigerator.
Hints: Buy sausages made from pure
beef or pork. They are tastier and less
fatty than the cheaper variety.
Honey Soy Marinade can also be used
over chicken, beef or lamb. Marinate
overnight for best results.

LAMB BURGER WITH MANGO, CILANTRO AND MINT SALSA

Preparation time: 30 minutes
Total cooking time: 10–15 minutes
Makes 8 patties

15 oz can mango slices
2 lb lean ground lamb
1 small red onion, finely chopped
1 tablespoon chopped fresh
   cilantro
1 egg
1 cup stale bread crumbs
2 tablespoons sweet chili sauce
1/4 teaspoon salt

Mango Salsa
1/2 small red onion, chopped
1 tablespoon chopped fresh mint
1 tablespoon chopped fresh
   cilantro
2/3 cup finely chopped cucumber
1 tablespoon white wine vinegar
1 small red chili, chopped
2 teaspoons sugar
salt and pepper to taste

➤ PREPARE AND HEAT barbecue. Lightly grease barbecue griddle. Drain mangoes, reserving 1 tablespoon syrup. Cut mangoes into 1/2 inch cubes.
1 Combine lamb, onion, cilantro, egg, bread crumbs, chili sauce and salt in bowl. Add 1/4 cup of the mango; mix until well combined. Divide into 8 portions. Shape into patties.
2 Place patties on hot, lightly oiled barbecue griddle. Cook 5 minutes each side or until cooked through. Serve with Mango Salsa.
3 To make Mango Salsa: Combine remaining mango and syrup with onion, herbs, cucumber, vinegar, chili, sugar, salt and pepper in bowl; mix well.

COOK'S FILE

Storage time: Patties can be prepared 1 day in advance and stored, covered, in refrigerator.
Hint: Salsa can also be served as a dip; mix with a little plain yogurt and serve with chunks of fresh bread.

HERB AND GARLIC SAUSAGES WITH RED ONION RELISH

Preparation time: 20 minutes
Total cooking time: 40 minutes
Serves 4

4 herb and garlic sausage links
10 inch square focaccia
4 lettuce leaves, shredded
1 medium tomato, sliced

Red Onion Relish
2 tablespoons olive oil
2 medium red onions, sliced
2 teaspoons balsamic vinegar
1 tablespoon sugar

➤ PREPARE AND HEAT barbecue.
1 Place sausages on hot, lightly oiled barbecue grill or griddle. Barbecue, turning frequently, 10 minutes or until well browned and cooked through. Cut sausages in half, lengthwise.
2 Cut focaccia into quarters, split in half horizontally and toast under pre-heated broiler each side until golden. Place lettuce and tomato on each focaccia base, followed by sausage. Top with Red Onion Relish. Cover with remaining focaccia squares. Serve with grilled peppers, if desired.
3 To make Red Onion Relish: Heat oil in medium pan, cook onions over medium-low heat 15 minutes, stirring frequently, until very soft but not browned. Add vinegar and sugar; cook a further 10 minutes. Serve warm or at room temperature.

COOK'S FILE

Storage time: Relish can be made up to 1 day in advance.
Hint: Use any of the wide variety of flavored sausages now available from butchers or some supermarkets.

Lamb Burger with Mango, Cilantro and Mint Salsa (top)
Herb and Garlic Sausage with Red Onion Relish.

SAUSAGE SKEWERS WITH QUICK TOMATO SAUCE

Preparation time: 25 minutes
Total cooking time: 35 minutes
Serves 4

4 beef sausage links
16 small button mushrooms
4 bacon slices
4 lamb kidneys, optional
2 tablespoons butter, melted
4 large tomatoes, halved

Quick Tomato Sauce
1 tablespoon oil
1 small onion, finely chopped
3 medium tomatoes, peeled,
    finely chopped
¼ cup barbecue sauce

➤ PREPARE AND HEAT barbecue.
1 Place sausages in a large pan, cover with cold water and bring slowly to simmering point. Leave to cool. Drain well and cut each sausage into six pieces.
2 Wipe mushrooms clean with paper towels. Chop bacon into bite-size pieces. If using kidneys, trim them, remove core and cut into quarters.
3 Thread sausage, bacon, kidney (if using) and mushrooms alternately on skewers. Place skewers on hot, lightly oiled barbecue griddle, brush with melted butter and cook 15 minutes, turning occasionally, or until browned and cooked through. Place tomatoes on hot grill cut-side down; cook 5 minutes. Serve skewers with tomatoes and Quick Tomato Sauce.
4 To make Quick Tomato Sauce: Heat oil in a small pan. Cook onion over medium-low heat 5 minutes until soft; add tomatoes and sauce. Cook 10 minutes, stirring occasionally. Serve warm or at room temperature.

COOK'S FILE

Storage time: Sauce can be made up to 1 day in advance.
Hints: If using wooden skewers, soak them in cold water 1 hour before assembling. This will help to prevent the wood from burning during cooking. Serve this dish with scrambled eggs and wholewheat English muffins for a hearty breakfast.

BARBECUED HOT DOGS WITH CREAMY SLAW

Preparation time: 20 minutes
Total cooking time: 10 minutes
Serves 6

6 large, thick, spicy
   frankfurters
1 tablespoon oil
6 hot dog buns
6 small lettuce leaves

Creamy Slaw
3 oz red cabbage
3 oz green cabbage
2 green onions
1/2 cup mayonnaise
1 tablespoon German mustard

➤ PREPARE AND HEAT barbecue.
1 Make 4 diagonal cuts in each frankfurter, slicing halfway through. Brush frankfurters with oil, and cook on hot, lightly oiled barbecue griddle 7–10 minutes or until cooked through.
2 Split buns lengthwise through the center top; line with lettuce leaf. Place Creamy Slaw on lettuce, and top with frankfurter. Serve immediately.
3 To make Creamy Slaw: Finely shred cabbage; finely chop green onions. Combine mayonnaise with mustard. Place all ingredients in medium mixing bowl and toss to combine thoroughly.

COOK'S FILE

Storage time: Slaw can be made up to 4 hours in advance. Barbecue frankfurters just before serving.

CHILI BURGER WITH AVOCADO SALSA

Preparation time: 25 minutes
Total cooking time: 10 minutes
Serves 6

2 lb lean ground beef
1 small onion, finely chopped
1 tablespoon chopped green chili
1 teaspoon ground cumin
2 tablespoons tomato paste
2 tablespoons chopped cilantro
6 bread rolls
6 lettuce leaves

Avocado Salsa
1 medium avocado
2 tablespoons lime juice
1 small tomato, chopped
1/2 cup cannned corn kernels,
   drained

➤ PREPARE AND HEAT barbecue. Place beef in a large mixing bowl.
1 Add onion, chili, cumin, tomato paste and cilantro. Using hands, mix until thoroughly combined. Divide mixture into 6 equal portions and shape into 1/2 inch thick patties.
2 Place patties on hot, lightly oiled grill or griddle. Barbecue 4–5 minutes each side, turning only once. Serve between split bread rolls with lettuce and Avocado Salsa.
3 To make Avocado Salsa: Peel avocado and remove pit. Cut into small cubes, place in a bowl and toss immediately with lime juice. Add tomato and corn and lightly combine.

COOK'S FILE

Storage time: Patties can be prepared up to 4 hours in advance.
Hint: Reduce the quantity of chili in this recipe to 2 teaspoons if you prefer a milder taste.

1

2

3

PORK SAUSAGE BURGER WITH MUSTARD CREAM

Preparation time: 20 minutes
Total cooking time: 15 minutes
Serves 6

2 lb lean ground pork
1 small onion, finely
   chopped
1 cup fresh bread crumbs
2 cloves garlic, crushed
1 egg, lightly beaten

1 teaspoon dried sage
6 long crusty bread rolls

Mustard Cream
1/2 cup sour cream
1 tablespoon wholegrain mustard
2 teaspoons lemon juice

➤ PREPARE AND HEAT barbecue. Place ground pork in large mixing bowl. **1** Add onion, bread crumbs, garlic, egg and sage. Using hands, mix to combine thoroughly. Divide the mixture into 6 equal portions, shape into sausage shapes about 6 inches long.
2 Place sausage burgers on hot, lightly oiled barbecue griddle or grill. Cook for 5–10 minutes, turning occasionally. Arrange burgers on long crusty rolls with Mustard Cream. Garnish with chives and serve with a salad, if desired.
3 To make Mustard Cream: Place sour cream, mustard and lemon juice in a small bowl and combine.

COOK'S FILE

Storage time: Burgers can be prepared up to 4 hours in advance.

1

2

3

CHEESE-STUFFED BURGER WITH RED SALSA

Preparation time: 25 minutes
+ 1 hour standing
Total cooking time: 20 minutes
Serves 6

2 lb lean ground beef
1 small onion, finely chopped
2 tablespoons chopped parsley
1 teaspoon dried oregano
1 tablespoon tomato paste
2 oz Monterey Jack cheese
6 sesame seed buns
lettuce leaves

Red Salsa
2 medium red peppers
1 medium ripe tomato, finely
   chopped
1 small red onion, finely
   chopped
1 tablespoon olive oil
2 teaspoons red wine vinegar

➤ PREPARE AND HEAT barbecue.
1 Place ground beef in large mixing bowl; add onion, herbs and tomato paste. Using hands, mix until thoroughly combined. Divide mixture into 6 equal portions and shape into patties. Cut cheese into small squares. Make a cavity in the top of each patty with thumb. Place cheese in cavity and smooth patty over to enclose the cheese completely.
2 Place patties on hot, lightly oiled barbecue grill or griddle. Barbecue 4–5 minutes each side, turning once. Remove from barbecue; keep warm. Split each bun in half; place a lettuce leaf on the base of each, top with patty and Red Salsa.
3 To make Red Salsa: Trim peppers, remove seeds and membrane.

Cut into wide pieces and place skin-side up under a hot broiler. Cook 4–5 minutes or until skin blisters and blackens. Cover with damp dish towel and leave to cool. Remove skin from peppers and finely chop flesh. Combine with tomato, onion, olive oil and vinegar and let stand at least 1 hour to allow flavors to develop. Serve salsa at room temperature.

COOK'S FILE

Storage time: Burgers can be prepared up to 4 hours in advance. Salsa can be made up to 1 day in advance. Store both, covered, in refrigerator.
Variation: Camembert, Brie or blue cheese can be used to stuff patties, if desired. Substitute bottled tomato sauce or ready-made salsa, available from supermarkets, if time is short.

1

2

3

shredded lettuce
2 tomatoes, thinly sliced
tomato sauce

➤ PREPARE AND HEAT barbecue.
1 Combine ground beef, onion, 1 egg, bread crumbs, tomato paste, Worcestershire sauce, parsley, salt and pepper in large bowl. Mix with hands until well combined.
2 Divide mixture into 6 portions. Shape each portion into round patties 1/2 inch thick. Cover and set aside. Slice onions into thin rings. Heat butter on hot barbecue griddle. Cook onions, turning often until well browned; move toward outer edge of griddle to keep warm. Brush barbecue grill or griddle liberally with oil.
3 Cook meat patties 3–4 minutes each side or until they are browned and cooked through. Move the patties to cooler part of barbecue or transfer them to a plate and keep warm. Place a slice of cheese on each patty. (The heat of the burger will be enough to partially melt the cheese.) Heat a small amount of butter in a large frying pan. Fry the 6 eggs and bacon until the eggs are cooked through and the bacon is golden and crisp. Remove from the heat.
To assemble burgers: Place the toasted bun bases on individual serving plates. Top each with lettuce and tomato. Place a cooked meat patty on top, followed by cooked onions, egg, bacon and tomato sauce. Place the remaining bun halves on top. Serve with french fries, if desired.

COOK'S FILE

Storage time: The burger patties can be prepared up to 4 hours in advance. Refrigerate until needed. Cook and assemble the burgers just before serving.

BURGER WITH THE WORKS

Preparation time: 40 minutes
Total cooking time: 10–15 minutes
Serves 6

1 1/2 lb lean ground beef
1 onion, finely chopped
1 egg
1/2 cup fresh bread crumbs
2 tablespoons tomato paste

1 tablespoon Worcestershire sauce
2 tablespoons chopped fresh parsley
salt and cracked pepper, to taste
3 large onions
2 tablespoons butter
6 slices cheddar cheese
6 large eggs
6 slices bacon
6 large hamburger buns, lightly toasted

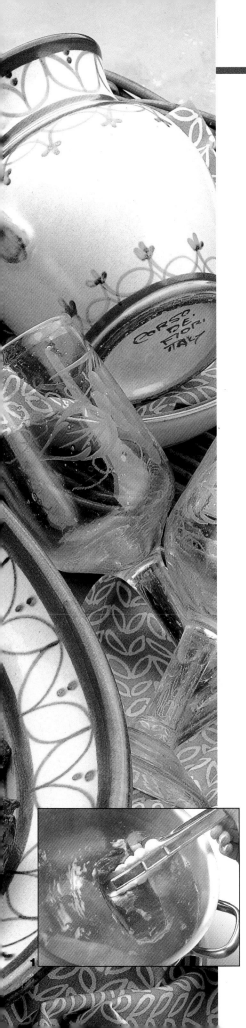

BEEF, LAMB & PORK

TANGY BEEF RIBS

Preparation time: 20 minutes
  + 3 hours marinating
Total cooking time: 15–20 minutes
Serves 4

2 lb beef ribs
1/2 cup tomato sauce
2 tablespoons Worcestershire
  sauce
2 tablespoons brown sugar
1 teaspoon paprika
1/4 teaspoon chili powder
1 clove garlic, crushed

➤ CHOP RIBS into individual serving pieces, if necessary. Bring a large pan of water to boil.
1 Place the ribs in the pan with the boiling water and cook for about 5 minutes then drain.
2 Combine the tomato sauce, Worcestershire sauce, brown sugar, paprika, chili powder and garlic in a large bowl and mix well. Add ribs to the Worcestershire sauce mixture and coat well. Cover and place in the refrigerator to marinate for several hours or preferably overnight. Prepare and heat the barbecue 1 hour before cooking.
3 Lightly grease the barbecue grill or griddle with oil, and cook the marinated ribs for about 10–15 minutes or until they are well browned and cooked right through. Brush the ribs frequently with the marinade during cooking. Serve with your favorite barbecued vegetables or slices of grilled fresh pineapple, if desired.

COOK'S FILE

Storage time: Ribs are best cooked just before serving.
Note: Ribs can be bought as a long piece or cut into individual pieces. If you are going to chop the ribs yourself you will need a sharp cleaver. Alternatively, the ribs can be cooked in one long piece and then carved into pieces after cooking, when the bone is softer. A longer cooking time will be required if ribs are cooked as a single piece.
Pork ribs can be used instead of beef ribs in this recipe. Use either the thick, meaty ribs, which are like beef ribs, or the long thin spare ribs. Pork spare ribs have less meat on them so less cooking is required. They can be eaten with the fingers, so are ideal picnic food.
Veal ribs are extremely tender and are sometimes available from specialty butchers. Ask your butcher to order them for you.

STEAK IN RED WINE

Preparation time: 10 minutes
 + 3 hours marinating
Total cooking time: 5–10 minutes
Serves 4

1¹/₂ lb round steak
1 cup good red wine
2 teaspoons garlic salt
1 tablespoon dried oregano
cracked black pepper, to taste

➤ CUT STEAKS into similar-sized serving pieces.

1 Trim meat of excess fat and sinew.

2 Combine wine, salt, oregano and pepper in a cup. Place steak in a large, shallow non-metal dish, pour the marinade over meat. Cover and refrigerate several hours or overnight. Prepare and heat barbecue 1 hour before cooking.

3 Cook steak on hot, lightly greased barbecue grill on griddle 3–4 minutes each side or until cooked as desired.

Brush with marinade frequently. Serve with potato salad and corn on the cob.

COOK'S FILE

Storage time: Steak is best cooked just before serving.

Hint: Choose a basting brush with pure bristles. Nylon bristles can melt in the heat and introduce an unpleasant flavor to cooked foods.

Variation: Substitute 2 tablespoons of fresh oregano for dried oregano, if desired.

HOT PEPPERED STEAKS WITH HORSERADISH SAUCE

Preparation time: 15 minutes
Total cooking time: 10 minutes
Serves 4

4 medium-sized sirloin steaks
    (about 1 1/2–2 lb total)
1/4 cup seasoned, cracked
    pepper

Horseradish Sauce
2 tablespoons brandy
1/4 cup beef stock
1/3 cup heavy cream
1 tablespoon prepared horseradish
1/2 teaspoon sugar
salt and pepper, to taste

➤ PREPARE AND HEAT barbecue. Lightly grease barbecue grill. Trim meat of excess fat and sinew.
1 Coat steaks on both sides with pepper, pressing it firmly into the meat.

2 Barbecue steaks 5–10 minutes until cooked as desired. Serve with Horseradish Sauce and steamed vegetables, such as crisp snow peas.
3 To make Horseradish Sauce: Combine brandy and stock in pan. Bring to boil, reduce heat. Stir in cream, horseradish and sugar and stir until heated through. Season to taste.

COOK'S FILE

Storage time: Steaks are best cooked just before serving.

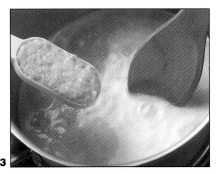

FILLET WITH FLAVORED BUTTERS

Preparation time: 30 minutes
Total cooking time: 15 minutes
Serves 4

4 beef tenderloin fillets
    (about 1–1½ lb total)

Garlic Butter
½ cup butter
3 cloves garlic, crushed
2 green onions, finely
    chopped

Red Pepper & Herb Butter
1 small red pepper
½ cup butter
2 teaspoons chopped oregano
2 teaspoons chopped chives
salt and pepper, to taste

➤ PREPARE AND HEAT barbecue. Lightly grease barbecue grill. Trim steaks of excess fat and sinew. Using a sharp knife, cut a pocket in the side of each steak.

1 **To make Garlic Butter:** Beat butter in bowl until creamy, add garlic and green onions; beat until smooth.

To make Red Pepper & Herb Butter: Cut pepper in half. Remove seeds and membrane. Place cut-side down on broiler rack. Brush skin with oil. Cook under preheated broiler until skin blisters and blackens. Remove from broiler. Cover with damp dish towel. Cool. Peel away skin and discard. Finely chop pepper flesh. Beat butter until creamy. Add red pepper, herbs, salt and pepper; beat until smooth.

2 Stuff 2–3 teaspoons of the Garlic Butter into two of the steaks; stuff 2–3 teaspoons Pepper & Herb Butter into remaining steaks.

3 Cook the steaks on hot barbecue grill or griddle 4–5 minutes each side, turning once. Brush frequently with any remaining flavored butter while cooking.

Storage time: Prepare steak 1 day in advance; store in refrigerator. Butters will keep 2 weeks in refrigerator, provided they are well covered.

BEEF SATAY WITH PEANUT SAUCE

Preparation time: 30 minutes
  + 3 hours marinating
Total cooking time: 10–15 minutes
Serves 4

1¹/2 lb round steak
¹/3 cup soy sauce
2 tablespoons oil
2 cloves garlic, crushed
1 teaspoon grated ginger

Peanut Sauce
1 cup pineapple juice
1 cup peanut butter
¹/2 teaspoon garlic powder

¹/2 teaspoon onion powder
2 tablespoons sweet chili sauce
¹/4 cup soy sauce

➤ TRIM STEAK of any excess fat and sinew.
1 Slice meat across the grain evenly into long, thin strips. Thread meat strips onto skewers, bunching them thickly along three-quarters of the skewer; place skewers in a shallow, non-metal dish.
2 Combine soy sauce, oil, garlic and ginger; pour over skewers. Store in refrigerator, covered with plastic wrap, several hours or overnight, turning occasionally. Prepare and heat barbecue 1 hour before cooking. Place skewers on hot, lightly oiled grill or griddle. Barbecue 8–10 minutes or until tender, turning occasionally. Serve with Peanut Sauce.
3 To make Peanut Sauce: Combine juice, peanut butter, garlic and onion powders and sauces in a small pan and stir over medium heat 5 minutes or until smooth. Serve warm.

COOK'S FILE

Storage time: Barbecue satay skewers just before serving. Sauce can be made 1 day in advance. If sauce has thickened, add a little warm water when reheating.
Variation: The quantity of chili sauce may be altered to taste. Alternatively, you can use chopped fresh chili peppers for extra spice.

LAMB CHOPS WITH ROSEMARY MARINADE

Preparation time: 15 minutes
  + 20 minutes marinating
Total cooking time: 6–8 minutes
Serves 4

12 lamb rib chops
¼ cup olive oil
2 tablespoons fresh chopped
   rosemary
1½ teaspoons cracked black
   pepper
1 bunch fresh rosemary

➤ PREPARE AND HEAT barbecue.
1 Trim chops of excess fat and sinew. Place chops in shallow, non-metal dish and brush with oil.
2 Scatter half the chopped rosemary and pepper on meat; set aside for 20 minutes. Turn meat over and brush with remaining oil, scatter over remaining rosemary and pepper. Tie the extra bunch of rosemary to the back of a wooden spoon.
3 Arrange chops on hot, lightly greased grill. Cook 2–3 minutes each side. As chops cook, pat frequently with the rosemary spoon. This will release flavorsome oils into the cutlets. When chops are almost done, remove rosemary from the spoon and drop it on the fire where it will flare up briefly and infuse rosemary smoke into the chops. Serve with barbecued lemon slices, if desired.

COOK'S FILE

Storage time: Cook chops just before serving.
Variation: This dish is ideal for a barbecue picnic. Marinate and pack in a sealed container with rosemary sprigs. Add sprigs to the fire, as described above.

LAMB CHOPS WITH PINEAPPLE SALSA

Preparation time: 20 minutes
Total cooking time: 10 minutes
Serves 6

12 lamb loin chops
2 tablespoons oil
1 teaspoon cracked black
    pepper

Pineapple Salsa
1/2 ripe pineapple (or 15¼ oz
    can pineapple tidbits)
1 large red onion
1 fresh red chili
1 tablespoon cider or rice wine
    vinegar
1 teaspoon sugar
salt and black pepper, to taste
2 tablespoons chopped mint

➤ PREPARE AND HEAT barbecue.
1 Trim meat of excess fat and sinew. Brush chops with oil and season with pepper.
2 To make Pineapple Salsa: Peel pineapple; remove core and eyes. Cut into 3/8 inch cubes. Peel onion, finely chop. Slit open chili, scrape out seeds. Chop chili flesh finely. Combine pineapple, onion and chili in medium bowl; mix lightly. Add vinegar, sugar, salt, pepper and mint; mix well.
3 Place lamb chops on lightly greased barbecue grill or griddle. Cook chops 2–3 minutes each side, turning once, until just tender. Serve with Pineapple Salsa, baked potatoes and green salad, if desired.

COOK'S FILE

Storage: Chops are best barbecued just before serving. Salsa can be made 1 day in advance and refrigerated. Add herbs just before serving. (Red onion may affect color of pineapple.)
Hint: Pineapple Salsa will also complement grilled tuna or salmon.

LAMB SATAY WITH CHILI PEANUT SAUCE

Preparation time: 25 minutes
  + 1 hour marinating
Total cooking time: 15 minutes
Serves 4

1¼ lb boneless lamb
2 cloves garlic, crushed
½ teaspoon ground black
    pepper
6 teaspoons finely chopped
    lemon grass
2 tablespoons soy sauce
2 teaspoons sugar
¼ teaspoon ground turmeric

Chili Peanut Sauce
1½ cups unsalted roasted
    peanuts
2 tablespoons vegetable oil
1 medium onion, coarsely
    chopped
1 clove garlic, coarsely chopped
1 tablespoon sambal oelek
    (or chopped fresh chilies)
1 tablespoon brown sugar
1 tablespoon kecap manis
    (sweet soy sauce) or soy sauce
1 teaspoon grated ginger
1½ teaspoons ground coriander
1 cup coconut milk
¼ teaspoon ground turmeric
salt and pepper, to taste

➤ TRIM LAMB of excess fat and sinew.

1 Cut lamb into thin strips. Thread onto skewers, bunching strips along three-quarters of the length. Place skewers in shallow non-metal dish. Combine garlic, pepper, lemon grass, soy sauce, sugar and turmeric in a small bowl; mix well. Brush marinade over skewered meat, set aside for 1 hour. Prepare and heat barbecue.

2 To make Chili Peanut Sauce: Process peanuts in food processor bowl 10 seconds or until coarsely ground. Heat oil in small pan. Add onion and garlic, cook over medium heat 3–4 minutes or until translucent. Add sambal oelek, sugar, kecap manis, ginger and coriander. Cook, stirring 2 minutes. Add coconut milk, turmeric and processed peanuts. Reduce heat, cook 3 minutes or until thickened; season with salt and pepper. Remove from heat.

3 Place mixture in food processor bowl. Process 20 seconds or until almost smooth. Spoon into individual serving dishes to cool. Barbecue

skewers on hot, lightly greased grill or griddle 2–3 minutes each side or until browned.

COOK'S FILE

Storage time: Barbecue satays just before serving. Satays can be marinated up to 2 days in advance. Store, covered, in refrigerator. Sauce can be made 3–4 days in advance. Store in a screwtop jar in refrigerator.
Variation: Salted roasted peanuts can be used in Chili Peanut Sauce. (Taste sauce before adding any additional salt.)
Hint: Chili Peanut Sauce can be used over any beef or vegetable satays.

1

2

3

LAMB KEFTA KABOBS WITH TAHINI DRESSING

Preparation time: 25 minutes
Total cooking time: 10 minutes
Serves 4–6

1¼ lb lean lamb
1 medium onion, coarsely
  chopped
2 cloves garlic, coarsely chopped
1 teaspoon cracked black
  pepper
1½ teaspoons ground cumin
½ teaspoon ground cinnamon
1 teaspoon sweet paprika
1 teaspoon salt
2 slices bread, crusts removed,
  quartered

1 egg, lightly beaten
olive oil, for coating

Tahini Dressing
2 tablespoons tahini (sesame
  paste)
1 tablespoon lemon juice
1 small garlic clove, crushed
salt to taste
2–3 tablespoons water
2 tablespoons sour cream
1 tablespoon chopped fresh
  parsley

➤ TRIM MEAT of any excess fat and sinew. Cut into small pieces suitable for processing. Prepare and heat the barbecue.

1 Place lamb, onion, garlic, pepper, cumin, cinnamon, paprika, salt, bread and egg in food processor bowl.

Process 20–30 seconds or until mixture becomes a smooth paste.

2 Divide mixture into 12. Using oil-coated hands, shape portions into sausages. Wrap sausages around skewers; refrigerate until needed.

To make Tahini Dressing: Combine tahini, lemon juice, garlic, salt, water, sour cream and parsley in small bowl. Stir until creamy.

3 Arrange kefta kabobs on hot, lightly greased barbecue grill or griddle. Cook 10 minutes, turning frequently, until browned and cooked through. Serve with Tahini Dressing and grilled tomato halves, if desired.

COOK'S FILE

Storage time: Cook kabobs just before serving. Tahini Dressing can be made 1 day in advance.

1

2

3

PORK LOIN CHOPS WITH APPLE CHUTNEY

Preparation time: 20 minutes
 + 3 hours marinating
Total cooking time: 25 minutes
Serves 6

6 pork loin chops
²⁄3 cup white wine
2 tablespoons oil
2 tablespoons honey
1¹⁄2 teaspoons ground
    cumin
2 cloves garlic, crushed

Apple Chutney
3 Granny Smith apples

1/2 cup apple juice
1/2 cup fruit chutney
1 tablespoon butter

➤ TRIM PORK CHOPS of excess fat and tendons.

1 Combine wine, oil, honey, cumin and garlic; mix well. Place chops in shallow non-metal dish; pour marinade over. Store, covered with plastic wrap, in refrigerator several hours or overnight, turning occasionally. Prepare and heat barbecue 1 hour before cooking.

2 Place chops on hot, lightly oiled barbecue grill or griddle. Cook 8 minutes each side or until tender, turning once. Serve immediately with Apple Chutney.

3 To make Apple Chutney: Peel apples and cut into small cubes. Place in small pan; cover with apple juice. Bring to boil, reduce heat and simmer, covered, 7 minutes or until completely soft. Add chutney and butter; stir to combine. Serve warm.

COOK'S FILE

Storage time: Pork chops can be marinated up to 1 day in advance. Barbecue just before serving. Apple Chutney can be made 1 day in advance. Store, covered, in refrigerator and reheat gently to serve.

Hint: Apple Chutney can be served with roast pork, lamb chops or chicken. It can also be served as a relish with a cheese plate. Serve warm or cold.

1

2

3

GINGER-ORANGE PORK CHOPS

Preparation time: 15 minutes
 + 3 hours marinating
Total cooking time: 20 minutes
Serves 6

6 pork butterfly chops
    (5 oz each)
1 cup ginger or white wine
1/2 cup orange marmalade
2 tablespoons oil
1 tablespoon grated ginger

➤ TRIM PORK CHOPS of excess fat and tendons.

1 Combine wine, marmalade, oil and ginger; mix well. Place chops in shallow non-metal dish; pour marinade over. Store, covered with plastic wrap, in refrigerator several hours or overnight, turning occasionally. Prepare and heat barbecue 1 hour before cooking. Drain pork chops; reserve marinade.

2 Place pork on hot, lightly oiled barbecue grill or griddle. Cook 5 minutes each side or until tender, turning once.

3 While the meat is cooking, place the reserved marinade in a small pan.

Bring to boil; reduce the heat and simmer for 5 minutes or until the marinade has reduced and thickened slightly. Pour the marinade over the pork chops immediately.

COOK'S FILE

Storage time: This recipe is best barbecued just before serving.

Hint: Chops of uneven thickness may curl during cooking. To prevent this, leave a layer of fat on the outside of the chop and make a few, deep cuts in the fat prior to cooking. Remove fat before serving.

1

2

3

Pork Loin Chops with Apple Chutney (top)
Ginger-Orange Pork Chops.

SWEET AND SOUR MARINATED PORK KABOBS

Preparation time: 30 minutes
   + 3 hours marinating
Total cooking time: 20 minutes
Serves 6

2 lb boneless pork
1 large red pepper
1 large green pepper
15$^{1}/_{4}$ oz can pineapple chunks
1 cup orange juice
$^{1}/_{4}$ cup white vinegar
2 tablespoons brown sugar
2 teaspoons chili garlic sauce
2 teaspoons cornstarch

➤ TRIM PORK of any excess fat and tendons.

1 Cut meat into 1 inch cubes. Cut both peppers into $^{3}/_{4}$ inch squares. Drain pineapple and reserve juice. Thread meat, alternating with peppers and pineapple, onto skewers. Combine reserved pineapple juice with orange juice, vinegar, sugar and sauce. Place kabobs in a shallow non-metal dish; pour over half the juice mixture over. Refrigerate, covered with plastic wrap, several hours or overnight, turning occasionally. Prepare and heat barbecue 1 hour before cooking.

2 To make Sweet and Sour Sauce: Place remaining marinade in small pan. Mix cornstarch with a tablespoon of the marinade in small bowl until smooth; add to pan. Stir over medium heat until mixture boils and thickens; transfer to small serving bowl. Cover surface with plastic wrap; leave to cool.

3 Place meat on a hot, lightly oiled barbecue grill or griddle. Cook 15 minutes, turning occasionally, until tender. Serve with Sweet and Sour Sauce.

COOK'S FILE

Storage time: Kabobs can be marinated up to 1 day in advance.
Note: Chili garlic sauce is readily available from Asian food shops and some supermarkets.

BARBECUED PORK SPARERIBS

Preparation time: 15 minutes
  + 3 hours marinating
Total cooking time: 30 minutes
Serves 4–6

4–6 lb pork spareribs
2 cups tomato sauce
1/2 cup sherry
2 tablespoons soy
  sauce
2 tablespoons honey
3 cloves garlic, crushed
1 tablespoon grated fresh
  ginger

➤ TRIM SPARERIBS of excess fat and sinew.

1 Cut racks of ribs into pieces, so that each piece has three or four ribs. Combine tomato sauce, sherry, soy sauce, honey, garlic and ginger in a large pan; mix well.

2 Add ribs to mixture. Bring to boil. Reduce heat and simmer, covered, 15 minutes. Move ribs occasionally to ensure even cooking. Transfer ribs and sauce to shallow non-metal dish; allow to cool. Refrigerate, covered with plastic wrap, several hours or overnight. Prepare and heat barbecue 1 hour before cooking.

3 Place ribs on hot, lightly oiled barbecue grill or griddle. Cook over the hottest part of the fire for 15 minutes, turning and brushing with sauce occasionally. Serve spareribs with barbecued corn on the cob and potato salad, if desired.

COOK'S FILE

Storage time: Ribs can be prepared up to 2 days in advance. Store, covered, in the refrigerator. Barbecue just before serving.

Note: Pork spareribs come in rack form. They can be eaten easily with the fingers if they are separated into individual ribs. Serve ribs with other pre-dinner finger foods next to a dipping sauce, such as barbecue or tomato, and a generous supply of napkins.

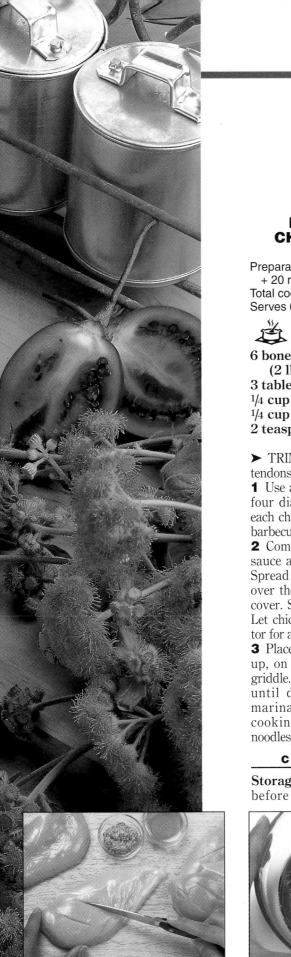

CHICKEN

HONEY-GLAZED CHICKEN BREASTS

Preparation time: 6 minutes
  + 20 minutes marinating
Total cooking time: 10 minutes
Serves 6

6 boneless chicken breasts
  (2 lb)
3 tablespoons butter, softened
1/4 cup honey
1/4 cup barbecue sauce
2 teaspoons seeded mustard

➤ TRIM CHICKEN of excess fat and tendons. Remove skin.

1 Use a sharp knife to make three or four diagonal slashes across top of each chicken breast. Prepare and heat barbecue.

2 Combine butter, honey, barbecue sauce and mustard in a small bowl. Spread half of the marinade thickly over the slashed side of the chicken; cover. Set remaining marinade aside. Let chicken marinate in the refrigerator for at least 20 minutes.

3 Place chicken breasts, slashed-side up, on hot, lightly greased grill or griddle. Cook 2–3 minutes each side or until done. Brush with reserved marinade several times during cooking. Serve hot with buttered noodles, if desired.

COOK'S FILE

Storage time: Barbecue chicken just before serving. Chicken can be marinated overnight, provided that it is kept, covered, in the refrigerator. The longer the chicken is marinated, the more it will take on flavor, so if chicken is preferred less sweet, marinate for a short time only.

Hints: Crisply fried onions are an appealing accompaniment to this dish. Peel 4 medium onions, cut in half and slice finely. Heat 4 cups of good quality vegetable oil or olive oil to medium-hot. Place onions in a frying basket, lower into the oil. (If oil begins to foam, lift basket out, set aside 30 seconds, then try again.) Cook for about 10–15 minutes or until onions are well browned and crisp. Drain on paper towels. Serve immediately.

Leftover cooked chicken can be shredded and tossed with a green salad or sliced thickly and made into sandwiches for a picnic.

Notes: When honey is cooked, its sugars caramelize and some of its flavor is lost. For a distinctive taste to this dish, use honeys with a strong, dark flavor, such as leatherwood, lavender or rosemary. Lighter honeys, such as yellow box, orange blossom or clover, will sweeten and glaze the meat without necessarily affecting its flavor. Usually the paler the honey, the milder its flavor.

If honey crystallizes, place the jar in a pan of warm water and turn gently until liquefied. Honey should be stored in a cool, dry place. (It will become grainy if refrigerated.)

THAI CHICKEN THIGHS

Preparation time: 20 minutes
  + 1 hour marinating
Total cooking time: 20 minutes
Serves 4–6

12 boneless chicken thighs
    (2$\frac{1}{2}$ lb)
6 cloves garlic
1 teaspoon black
    peppercorns
3 cilantro leaves and stems,
    coarsely chopped
$\frac{1}{4}$ teaspoon salt

Chili Garlic Dip
4–5 dried red chilies
2 large cloves garlic, chopped
$\frac{1}{4}$ cup sugar
$\frac{1}{3}$ cup rice wine vinegar
pinch salt
$\frac{1}{4}$ cup boiling water

➤ PREPARE AND HEAT barbecue.
1 Trim the chicken thighs of excess fat and tendons. Remove skin.
2 Place garlic, peppercorns, cilantro and salt in food processor bowl. Process 20–30 seconds or until the mixture forms a smooth paste. (This can also be done using a mortar and pestle.) Place chicken in shallow non-metal dish. Spread garlic mixture over chicken. Stand chicken at room temperature 1 hour.
3 To make Chili Garlic Dip: Soak chilies in hot water 20 minutes. Drain chilies and chop finely. Place in a mortar with garlic and sugar. Grind to a smooth paste. Place mixture in a small pan. Add vinegar, salt and water. Bring to boil, reduce heat, simmer 2–3 minutes. Cool.
4 Barbecue chicken on hot, greased grill or griddle 5–10 minutes each side, turning once. Serve with Chili Garlic Dip.

COOK'S FILE

Storage: Chicken can be marinated, in refrigerator, 1 day in advance. Dip can be made 3 days in advance.
Hint: Serve chicken with a salad of sliced cucumber and shredded carrot and radish marinated in rice wine vinegar, sugar and salt. The sweet-tart flavor of the salad complements the spiciness of the chicken.

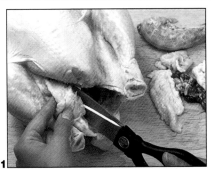

MIDDLE EASTERN BAKED CHICKEN

Preparation time: 30 minutes
Total cooking time: 1 hour 15 minutes
Serves 6

3¹/4 lb whole chicken
¹/2 cup boiling water
¹/2 cup instant couscous
4 pitted dates, chopped
4 dried apricots, chopped
1 tablespoon lime juice
1 tablespoon olive oil
1 tablespoon butter
1 medium onion, chopped
1–2 cloves garlic, chopped
1 teaspoon salt
¹/4 teaspoon cracked black pepper
1 teaspoon ground coriander
2 tablespoons chopped parsley
salt and pepper, extra
1 teaspoon ground cumin
1 tablespoon olive oil

➤ PREPARE AND HEAT kettle barbecue for indirect cooking. (See page 7.) Place drip pan underneath top rack.

1 Remove giblets and any large deposits of fat from chicken. Wipe or pat chicken dry with paper towel. Pour boiling water over couscous and set aside 15 minutes to swell and soften. Soak dates and apricots in lime juice; set aside.

2 Heat oil and butter in pan, add onion and garlic; cook 3–4 minutes until translucent. Remove from heat; add couscous and soaked dried fruit, salt, pepper, coriander and parsley. Mix well. Spoon stuffing into chicken cavity and close with toothpicks or a skewer. Tie legs together with string.

3 Rub chicken skin all over with combined salt, pepper, cumin and extra oil. Place chicken in the center of a large piece of greased foil. Gather edges of foil and wrap securely.

4 Place the parcel on barbecue rack over drip pan. Cover barbecue, cook 50 minutes. Open the foil, crimping the edges to form a tray to retain most of the cooking liquids. Cook 20 min-

utes more or until chicken is tender, golden and the juices run clear. Remove from heat and stand 5–6 minutes before carving.

COOK'S FILE

Storage: Stuffing can be prepared 3–4 hours in advance. Bake and stuff chicken just before serving.

Hint: Leftover chicken can be sliced and served with a salad of avocado, sliced onion and orange segments.

CHICKEN THIGHS WITH CORN RELISH

Preparation time: 20 minutes
Total cooking time: 25 minutes
Serves 4

8 chicken thighs,
   skin on (2 lb)
1 tablespoon olive oil
1 small clove garlic, crushed
1/4 teaspoon ground turmeric
1/2 teaspoon salt

Corn Relish
1 cup frozen or canned corn
   kernels
1 tablespoon olive oil
1 red chili, seeded and chopped
1 small green pepper finely
   chopped
1 medium onion, finely chopped
1/3 cup white vinegar
1/4 cup sugar
1 teaspoon seeded mustard
1/2 cup water
1 tablespoon cornstarch
1 teaspoon paprika
1 teaspoon finely chopped fresh
   cilantro
1 tablespoon olive oil

➤ PREPARE AND HEAT barbecue. Trim chicken of excess fat and tendons.
1 Prick skin of chicken thighs with point of a knife and place in large frying pan of boiling water. Reduce heat, simmer 5 minutes. Remove from pan; drain. Cool. Combine olive oil, garlic, turmeric and salt and rub over the skin of the thighs. Set aside.
2 To make Corn Relish: Cook corn in pan of boiling water 2–3 minutes or until tender; drain. (If using canned corn, drain, but do not cook.) Heat oil in medium pan. Add chili, pepper and onion. Cook over medium heat until tender. Add corn, vinegar, sugar and mustard, and cook, stirring, a further 5 minutes. Add blended water and cornstarch. Bring to boil, reduce heat, stir until thickened. Stir in paprika, cilantro and remaining extra oil. Remove from heat; cool.
3 Place thighs, skin-side up, on hot, lightly greased barbecue grill or flatplate. Cook 2 minutes, turn and cook skin-side down 4 minutes. Continue cooking another 5–10 minutes, turning frequently until the chicken is well browned and cooked through. Serve with Corn Relish.

COOK'S FILE

Storage time: Relish can be made up to 4 days in advance, stored in a jar and refrigerated.

CHICKEN KABOBS WITH CURRY MAYONNAISE

Preparation time: 25 minutes
  + 30 minutes marinating
Total cooking time: 10 minutes
Serves 4

1¼ lb boneless chicken breast
  fillets
4 large green onions
1 small green pepper
1 small red pepper
¼ cup olive oil
1 teaspoon freshly ground black
  pepper
½ teaspoon ground turmeric
1½ teaspoons ground coriander

Curry Mayonnaise
¾ cup mayonnaise
1 tablespoon hot curry powder
¼ cup sour cream
1 tablespoon sweet fruit or
  mango chutney, mashed
¼ cup finely chopped, peeled
  cucumber
½ teaspoon toasted cumin seeds
1 tablespoon finely chopped
  fresh mint
1 teaspoon finely chopped fresh
  mint for garnish

➤ PREPARE AND HEAT barbecue. Remove skin, excess fat and tendons from chicken.

1 Cut chicken into 1½ inch cubes. Trim green onions, cut white stems and thicker parts of green stems into 1¼ inch lengths; discard tops. Cut peppers into 1½ inch squares.

2 Thread the chicken, green onions and red and green pepper squares onto skewers, using at least two pieces of each. Arrange the kabobs, side by side, in a shallow, non-metal dish. Combine the oil, pepper, turmeric and coriander. Pour the mixture over the kabobs; set aside for 30 minutes at room temperature.

3 To make Curry Mayonnaise: Combine mayonnaise, curry powder, sour cream, chutney, cucumber, cumin seeds and mint in a bowl; mix well. Spoon into a dish for serving. Sprinkle mayonnaise with extra chopped mint. Place kabobs on hot, lightly oiled barbecue grill or griddle. Cook 2–3 minutes each side or until cooked through and tender. Serve Curry Mayonnaise separately.

COOK'S FILE

Storage time: Kabobs can be assembled 4 hours in advance. Mayonnaise can be made 1 day in advance and stored in refrigerator. Sprinkle with extra mint just before serving.

Hint: Serve chicken kabobs with rice and fried pappadums, or wrapped in pita bread.

CITRUS CHICKEN DRUMSTICKS

Preparation time: 20 minutes
+ 3 hours marinating
Total cooking time: 20 minutes
Serves 4

8 chicken drumsticks
1/3 cup orange juice
1/3 cup lemon juice
1 teaspoon grated orange rind
1 teaspoon grated lemon rind
1 teaspoon sesame oil
1 tablespoon olive oil
1 green onion, finely chopped

➤ WASH DRUMSTICKS and pat dry with paper towels.

1 Trim any excess fat and score thickest part of chicken with a knife. Place in a shallow non-metal dish.

2 Combine juices, rinds, oils and green onion, pour over chicken. Store, covered with plastic wrap, in refrigerator several hours or overnight, turning occasionally. Drain chicken, reserve marinade. Prepare and heat barbecue 1 hour before cooking.

3 Cook drumsticks on hot, lightly oiled barbecue grill or griddle for 15–20 minutes or until tender and no longer pink. Brush occasionally with the reserved marinade. Serve immediately.

C O O K ' S   F I L E

Storage time: This dish is best cooked just before serving.

1

2

3

BARBECUED TANDOORI CHICKEN

Preparation time: 15 minutes
+ 4 hours marinating
Total cooking time: 1 hour
Serves 4

4 chicken quarters, skin removed
1 teaspoon salt
2 cloves garlic, crushed
1 tablespoon lemon juice
1 cup plain yogurt
1 1/2 teaspoons garam masala
1/2 teaspoon ground black pepper
1/2 teaspoon ground turmeric
2–3 drops red food coloring
olive oil, for basting
20–30 mesquite or hickory chips, for smoking

➤ PLACE CHICKEN in a non-metal dish; rub with salt and garlic.

1 Combine lemon juice, yogurt, garam masala, pepper and turmeric. Add food coloring to make the marinade a bright orange-red color. Pour over the chicken, and coat evenly with the back of a spoon. Cover and refrigerate 4 hours, turning chicken every hour to redistribute the marinade. During last hour of marinating, heat and prepare kettle barbecue for indirect cooking (see page 7) and soak wood chips.

2 When barbecue coals are covered with fine white ash, add drained mesquite or hickory chips. Cover the barbecue and leave until the smoke is well established (about 5 minutes).

3 Brush barbecue grill with oil. Arrange chicken on grill; put lid on barbecue. Smoke-cook 45 minutes–1 hour or until chicken is well crisped. Brush chicken with oil several times during cooking. Serve with side salad and onion rings, if desired.

C O O K ' S   F I L E

Storage time: Cook the chicken just before serving.
Note: Tandoori chicken requires a slow heat. Do not place chicken on barbecue while the fire is still very hot. Test the heat of the fire before adding the chips. Hold your hand over the top rack. If you can leave your hand, comfortably, for 4–5 seconds the fire is low enough to use. If fire is too hot, allow to burn down for 15–30 minutes more.

1

2

3

Citrus Chicken Drumsticks (top)
Barbecued Tandoori Chicken.

BUFFALO CHICKEN WINGS WITH RANCH DRESSING

Preparation time: 25 minutes
  + 3 hours marinating
Total cooking time: 10 minutes
Serves 4

2 lb chicken wings
2 teaspoons black pepper
2 teaspoons garlic salt
2 teaspoons onion powder
olive oil, for deep frying
1/2 cup tomato sauce
2 tablespoons Worcestershire
  sauce
2 tablespoons butter, melted
2 teaspoons sugar
Tabasco sauce, to taste

Ranch Dressing
1/2 cup mayonnaise
1/2 cup sour cream
2 tablespoons lemon juice
2 tablespoons chopped chives
salt and white pepper, to taste

➤ WASH WINGS thoroughly and pat dry with paper towels

1 Cut tips off each wing; discard. Bend each wing back to snap joint and cut through to create two pieces. Combine pepper, garlic salt and onion powder. Using fingers, rub mixture into each piece.

2 Heat oil to moderately hot in deep heavy-based pan. Cook chicken pieces in batches 2 minutes; remove with tongs or slotted spoon and drain on paper towels.

3 Transfer chicken to non-metal bowl or shallow dish. Combine sauces, butter, sugar and Tabasco and pour over chicken; stir to coat. Refrigerate, covered, several hours or overnight. Prepare and heat barbecue 1 hour before cooking.

4 Place chicken on hot, lightly oiled barbecue grill or griddle. Cook 5 minutes, turning and brushing with marinade. Serve with Ranch Dressing.

To make Ranch Dressing: Combine mayonnaise, sour cream, juice, chives, salt and pepper in bowl; mix well.

COOK'S FILE

Storage time: Wings can be prepared up to 2 days in advance.

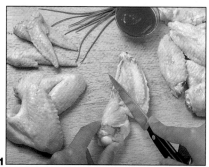

CHICKEN BURGER WITH TARRAGON MAYONNAISE

Preparation time: 25 minutes
Total cooking time: 20 minutes
Serves 6

2 lb lean ground chicken
1 small onion, finely chopped
2 teaspoons lemon rind
2 tablespoons sour cream
1 cup fresh bread crumbs
6 onion rolls

Tarragon Mayonnaise
1 egg yolk or 2 tablespoons egg
    substitute
1 tablespoon tarragon vinegar
1/2 teaspoon Dijon mustard
1 cup olive oil
salt and white pepper, to taste

➤ PREPARE AND HEAT barbecue.
1 Place ground chicken in a mixing bowl. Add onion, rind, sour cream and bread crumbs. Using hands, mix until thoroughly combined. Divide mixture into 6 equal portions and shape into 1/2 inch thick patties.
2 Place patties on hot, lightly oiled barbecue grill or griddle. Cook 7 minutes each side, turning once. Serve on an onion roll with salad fillings and Tarragon Mayonnaise.
3 To make Tarragon Mayonnaise: Place yolk or egg substitute, half the vinegar and the mustard in a small mixing bowl. Whisk together 1 minute until light and creamy. Add oil about 1 teaspoon at a time, whisking constantly until mixture thickens. Increase flow of oil to a thin stream; continue whisking until all the oil has been incorporated. Stir in remaining vinegar and salt and white pepper.

COOK'S FILE

Storage time: Burgers can be prepared up to 1 day in advance and mayonnaise up to 4 hours in advance. Store both in refrigerator.
Variation: Mayonnaise can also be made in a food processor. Add the oil in a thin stream, with the motor running, until the mixture thickens and turns creamy.
Note: Do not use black pepper in mayonnaise as mixture may discolor.

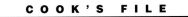

CHICKEN BREASTS WITH FRUIT MEDLEY

Preparation time: 25 minutes
 + 3 hours marinating
Total cooking time: 20 minutes
Serves 4

4 boneless chicken breasts,
   skin removed
3/4 cup white wine
1/4 cup olive oil
2 teaspoons grated
   ginger
1 clove garlic,
   crushed

Fruit Medley
8 oz can pineapple tidbits, drained
1 small mango, peeled
2 small kiwi fruit, peeled
6 oz watermelon, peeled, seeds
   removed
1 tablespoon finely chopped
   fresh mint

➤ TRIM CHICKEN of fat and tendons.
1 Place chicken in shallow non-metal dish. Combine wine, oil, ginger and garlic; pour over chicken. Refrigerate, covered with plastic wrap, several hours or overnight, turning occasionally. Prepare and light barbecue 1 hour before cooking.

2 Place chicken on hot, lightly oiled barbecue grill or griddle. Cook for 5–10 minutes each side, or until well browned. Serve immediately with Fruit Medley and barbecued onion slices, if desired.
3 To make Fruit Medley: Chop fruit finely and combine with mint in small serving bowl.

COOK'S FILE

Storage time: Chicken can be marinated up to 2 days in advance.
Variation: Use any of your favorite fruits in season for the Fruit Medley. Use at least one ingredient with a firm flesh, for example, an apple or a pear.

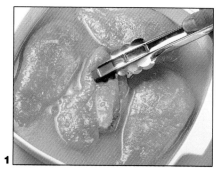

TANDOORI SKEWERS

Preparation time: 20 minutes
 + 3 hours marinating
Total cooking time: 10 minutes
Serves 4–6

2 lb boneless chicken thighs,
   skin removed
1 cup plain yogurt
1 teaspoon chili powder
1 teaspoon turmeric
1 teaspoon ground cumin
1 teaspoon ground
   coriander

1 teaspoon grated ginger
1 clove garlic, crushed

➤ TRIM CHICKEN of excess fat and tendons.
1 Cut each thigh into thin strips; weave onto small skewers, bunching the chicken along about three-quarters of the length.
2 Combine yogurt, spices, ginger and garlic; mix well. Place skewers in shallow non-metal dish, cover with yogurt mixture and refrigerate, covered with plastic wrap, several hours or overnight, turning occasionally. Prepare and heat barbecue 1 hour before cooking.

3 Place chicken on hot, lightly oiled barbecue grill or griddle. Cook for 8–10 minutes or until tender.

COOK'S FILE

Storage time: Skewers can be marinated up to 2 days in advance and cooked just before serving.
Note: Thighs are dark meat and will remain slightly pink even when cooked. To ensure that the chicken cooks evenly, do not bunch the meat too tightly on the skewer. Test chicken for doneness by removing from heat and piercing to the middle with a skewer. Chicken is done when juices run clear.

Chicken Breasts with Fruit Medley (top)
Tandoori Skewers.

TERIYAKI CHICKEN WINGS

Preparation time: 15 minutes
  + 3 hours marinating
Total cooking time: 13 minutes
Serves 4

8 chicken wings
¼ cup soy sauce
2 tablespoons sherry
2 teaspoons grated ginger
1 clove garlic, crushed
1 tablespoon honey

➤ WASH CHICKEN wings and pat dry with paper towel.

1 Trim any excess fat from wings, and tuck tips under to form a triangle.

2 Place the wings in shallow non-metal dish. Combine the soy sauce, sherry, ginger, garlic and honey; mix well. Pour over the chicken. Store, covered with plastic wrap, in refrigerator several hours or overnight. Prepare and light barbecue 1 hour before cooking. Lightly brush two sheets of aluminum foil with oil. Place 4 wings in a single layer on each piece of foil; wrap completely.

3 Place foil packets on hot barbecue grill or griddle for 10 minutes, then remove from heat and unwrap. Place wings directly on lightly greased grill 3 minutes or until brown. Turn wings frequently and brush with any remaining marinade.

COOK'S FILE

Storage time: Chicken can be marinated up to 2 days in advance. Cook just before serving.

Variation: Marinade can also be used on beef or pork.

Note: Teriyaki marinade is available in the Asian section of most supermarkets or Asian food shops.

CHICKEN FAJITAS

Preparation time: 35 minutes
  + 3 hours marinating
Total cooking time: 10 minutes
Serves 4

4 boneless chicken breasts,
  skin removed
2 tablespoons olive oil
1/4 cup lime juice
2 cloves garlic, crushed
1 teaspoon ground cumin
1/4 cup chopped fresh cilantro
8 flour tortillas
1 tablespoon olive oil, extra
2 medium onions, sliced

2 medium green peppers, cut
  into thin strips
1 cup grated Monterey Jack
  cheese
1 large avocado, sliced
1 cup bottled tomato salsa

➤ TRIM CHICKEN of fat and tendons.
1 Cut chicken into thin strips. Place in shallow non-metal dish. Combine oil, juice, garlic, cumin and cilantro; mix well. Pour over chicken. Store, covered, in the refrigerator several hours or overnight. Prepare and heat barbecue 1 hour before cooking.
2 Wrap tortillas in foil and place on a cooler part of the barbecue grill for 10 minutes to warm through. Heat oil on griddle. Cook onion and pepper for 5 minutes or until soft. Push over to a cooler part of the grill to keep warm.
3 Place chicken and marinade on griddle and cook 5 minutes until just tender. Transfer chicken, vegetables and wrapped tortillas to serving platter. Make up individual fajitas by placing chicken, cooked onion and pepper, grated cheese and avocado over flat tortillas. Top with salsa and roll up.

COOK'S FILE

Storage time: Chicken can be marinated up to 2 days in advance.
Note: Tomato salsa is available from supermarkets and comes in hot, medium or mild forms.

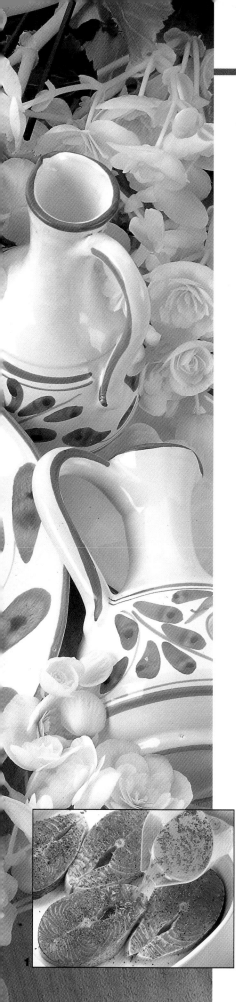

SEAFOOD

SALMON STEAKS WITH FRUIT SALSA

Preparation time: 20 minutes
 + 3 hours marinating
Total cooking time: 10 minutes
Serves 4

4 salmon steaks
2 tablespoons seasoned
    pepper
2 tablespoons lemon juice
1/2 cup lime juice
1 tablespoon chopped fresh
    thyme

Fruit Salsa
1/2 small papaya, peeled
1/4 small pineapple, peeled
3 green onions, chopped
1 tablespoon chopped fresh
    cilantro
2 tablespoons lime juice
1 tablespoon sugar
salt, to taste

➤ SPRINKLE SALMON steaks all over with seasoned pepper.
1 Place salmon in shallow non-metal dish. Combine lemon juice, lime juice and thyme; pour over salmon steaks. Cover and refrigerate several hours.
2 Place salmon on hot, lightly greased barbecue grill or griddle; brush with any remaining marinade. Cook 5–10 minutes each side, turning once, until outside is lightly browned and flesh is just cooked on the inside. Serve with Fruit Salsa.

3 To make Fruit Salsa: Chop papaya and pineapple into 3/8 inch cubes. Combine in medium bowl with green onions, cilantro, lime juice, sugar and salt.

COOK'S FILE

Storage time: Barbecue salmon just before serving. Do not marinate for more than 3 hours as the citrus juices will begin to "cook" the fish and turn the flesh opaque. If this should occur reduce the cooking time by half. Salsa should be made just before serving.
Notes: Salmon steaks can be expensive, so choose only the very best. Look for steaks with bright-orange flesh, that are firm to the touch, with a clear, dry bone. The skin should be pale gray.
When purchasing papaya look for a deep yellow skin color and a firm flesh. (If papaya yields easily to gentle pressure in the thickest area, it is over-ripe and should not be used.)
Smaller papayas with orange-red flesh (sometimes known as Mountain Papayas) are generally available at the beginning of summer. Their flesh is more delicate than the large variety.
Store uncut, ripe papayas in the refrigerator up to 7 days. Serve as soon as possible after cutting. Leftover papaya flesh can be peeled and chopped, covered with lemon juice, and stored in the refrigerator for up to 3 days. Alternatively, purée remaining flesh and freeze in icecube trays to use in fruit drinks.

CAJUN CALAMARI

Preparation time: 15 minutes
+ 3 hours marinating
Total cooking time: 5 minutes
Serves 4

1 1/4 lb large calamari
    (or squid) hoods
1/4 cup lemon juice
2 cloves garlic, crushed
2 teaspoons tomato paste
1 teaspoon garam masala
2 teaspoons ground coriander
2 teaspoons paprika
2 teaspoons seasoned pepper
2 teaspoons sugar
1 tablespoon grated
    fresh ginger
1 tablespoon olive oil
1/4 teaspoon ground nutmeg
pinch chili powder

➤ WASH CALAMARI thoroughly, removing any membrane. Pat dry with paper towel.

1 Using a sharp knife, cut through one side of each hood, open out to give a large, flat piece of flesh. With inside facing up, score flesh diagonally, in a criss-cross pattern, taking care not to cut all the way through. Against the grain of those cuts, slice flesh into long strips about 3/4 inch thick.

2 Combine juice, garlic, tomato paste, spices, sugar, ginger, oil, nutmeg and chili in bowl; mix well. Add calamari strips; stir to combine. Cover and refrigerate several hours or overnight. Prepare and heat barbecue 1 hour before cooking.

3 Cook calamari and marinade on hot, lightly greased barbecue griddle 5 minutes or until flesh curls and turns white. Remove from the heat and serve immediately.

COOK'S FILE

Storage time: The calamari can be marinated up to 2 days in advance.

1

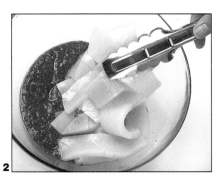

2

3

LEMON AND HERB TROUT

Preparation time: 20 minutes
Total cooking time: 15 minutes
Serves 4

1/4 cup chopped fresh dill
2 tablespoons chopped fresh
   rosemary
1/3 cup coarsely chopped fresh
   flat-leaf parsley
2 teaspoons thyme leaves
2 tablespoons crushed green
   peppercorns
1/3 cup lemon juice
salt and pepper, to taste
1 lemon
4 whole fresh trout
1/3 cup dry white wine

Horseradish Cream
1 tablespoon prepared horseradish
1/2 cup sour cream
2 tablespoons heavy cream
salt and pepper, to taste

Lemon Sauce
2 egg yolks
2/3 cup butter, melted
3–4 tablespoons lemon juice
salt and pepper, to taste

➤ PREPARE AND HEAT barbecue. Lightly grease four large sheets of foil, each double-thickness.

1 Combine herbs, peppercorns, juice, salt and pepper in bowl; mix well. Cut lemon into 8 slices, cut each slice in half. Place 2 lemon pieces in each fish cavity. Keep remaining lemon for another use. Spoon herb mixture into fish cavity.

2 Place each fish on foil layers, sprinkle each with 1 tablespoon of wine. Seal fish in foil to form neat bundles. Cook fish on barbecue 10–15 minutes or until fish is just cooked through.

(Test fish for doneness by gently flaking flesh with a fork.) Leave fish, wrapped in foil, 5 minutes, then serve with Horseradish Cream and Lemon Sauce. Garnish with limes and chives.

3 To make Horseradish Cream: Combine horseradish, sour cream, cream and salt and pepper; mix well.

To make Lemon Sauce: Place yolks in food processor. Process for

20 seconds. With motor running, add hot butter slowly in a thin, steady stream. Continue processing until all butter has been added and mixture is thick and creamy. Add juice; season with salt and pepper.

COOK'S FILE

Storage time: Prepare fish bundles 1 day in advance; store in refrigerator.

1

2

3

GARLIC SHRIMP

Preparation time: 10 minutes
  + 3 hours marinating
Total cooking time: 5 minutes
Serves 4

1 lb jumbo shrimp

Marinade
2 tablespoons lemon juice
2 tablespoons sesame oil
2 cloves garlic, crushed
2 teaspoons grated fresh
  ginger

➤ REMOVE HEADS from shrimp.
1 Peel and devein, leaving the tails intact. (Reserve the heads and shell for fish stock) Make a cut in the shrimp body, slicing three-quarters of the way through the flesh from head to tail as if butterflying.
To make Marinade: Combine juice, oil, garlic and ginger; mix well.
2 Place shrimp in bowl; pour on marinade and mix well. Cover and refrigerate several hours or overnight. Prepare and light barbecue 1 hour before cooking.
3 Cook shrimp on hot, lightly greased griddle for 3–5 minutes or until pink in color and cooked through. Brush frequently with marinade while cooking. Serve immediately.

COOK'S FILE

Storage time: Shrimp are best barbecued close to serving. Shrimp should always be cooked and eaten within 24 hours of purchase.
Variation: For a stronger garlic flavor, double the quantity of garlic and omit the ginger, if preferred. For a hot and spicy dish, substitute 2 finely chopped fresh chilies for the garlic.

1

2

3

CHARGRILLED BABY OCTOPUS

Preparation time: 15 minutes
  + 3 hours marinating
Total cooking time: 5 minutes
Serves 4

2 lb baby octopus
3/4 cup red wine
2 tablespoons balsamic
   vinegar
2 tablespoons soy sauce

2 tablespoons hoisin sauce
1 clove garlic, crushed

➤ WASH OCTOPUS thoroughly and wipe dry with paper towel.
1 Use a small sharp knife to slit open the head; remove the gut. Grasp the body firmly and push the beak out with your index finger. Remove and discard beak. If octopus are large, cut tentacles in half.
2 Place the octopus in large bowl. Combine the wine, vinegar, sauces and garlic; pour over octopus and stir

to coat completely. Cover and refrigerate several hours or overnight. Prepare and heat the barbecue 1 hour before cooking.
3 Drain octopus; reserve marinade. Cook octopus on hot, lightly greased griddle for 3–5 minutes until octopus flesh turns white. Pour over the reserved marinade while cooking. Serve warm or cold.

COOK'S FILE

Storage time: The octopus can be marinated up to 2 days in advance.

1

2

3

HONEYED SHRIMP AND SCALLOP SKEWERS

Preparation time: 15 minutes
   + 3 hours marinating
Total cooking time: 5 minutes
Makes 8 skewers

1 lb medium shrimp
8 oz fresh scallops
   with corals intact
1/4 cup honey
2 tablespoons soy sauce
1/4 cup bottled barbecue sauce
2 tablespoons sherry

➤ SOAK EIGHT WOODEN skewers in water.

1 Remove the heads from shrimp. Peel and devein, keeping the tails intact. Clean the scallops, removing the brown vein.

2 Thread the shrimp and scallops alternately onto 8 skewers (about 3 of each per skewer). Place a shallow non-metal dish. Combine honey, sauces and sherry and pour over skewers. Cover and refrigerate several hours or overnight. Prepare and heat barbecue 1 hour before cooking.

3 Cook skewers on hot lightly greased barbecue griddle for 5 minutes or until cooked through. Brush frequently with marinade while cooking.

C O O K ' S   F I L E

Storage time: Store marinated skewers in refrigerator for up to 2 days. Cook just before serving.
Variation: Substitute cubes of firm-fleshed fish for shrimp or scallops.

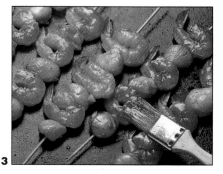

FISH PATTIES

Preparation time: 25 minutes
Total cooking time: 10 minutes
Makes 8–10 patties

1 1/2 lb white fish fillets, cut into
   cubes
1 cup stale white bread crumbs
3 green onions, chopped
1/4 cup lemon juice
2 teaspoons seasoned pepper
1 tablespoon chopped fresh dill
2 tablespoons chopped fresh
   parsley
3/4 cup grated cheddar cheese
1 egg
1/2 cup all-purpose flour, for
   dusting

Herbed Mayonnaise
1/2 cup mayonnaise
1 tablespoon chopped fresh
   parsley
1 tablespoon chopped fresh
   chives
2 teaspoons chopped capers

➤ PREPARE AND HEAT barbecue. Place the fish fillets in a food processor bowl. Process for 20–30 seconds or until smooth.

1 Place ground fish in large bowl. Add bread crumbs, green onions, juice, pepper, herbs, cheese and egg. Mix well. Divide into 8–10 portions. Shape into round patties. Place on tray and refrigerate 15 minutes or until firm.

2 Toss patties in flour, shake off excess. Cook on hot, lightly greased barbecue griddle 2–3 minutes each side until browned and cooked through. Serve Fish Patties with Herbed Mayonnaise and a green salad, if desired.

3 To make Herbed Mayonnaise: Combine the mayonnaise, herbs and capers in a small bowl; mix well.

C O O K ' S   F I L E

Storage time: This recipe is best made just before cooking. Patties should not be prepared more than a few hours in advance. After 2–3 hours the raw fish will begin to seep liquid which will cause the patties to fall apart during cooking.
Variation: Any firm-fleshed fish can be used in this recipe. Try whiting, perch, hake or cod.

Honeyed Shrimp and Scallop Skewers (top)
Fish Patties.

THAI MARINATED FISH

Preparation time: 10 minutes
  + 3 hours marinating
Total cooking time: 15 minutes
Serves 4

1 medium white-fleshed fish,
  cleaned and scaled
3/4 cup fresh cilantro
2 cloves garlic, crushed
1 tablespoon soy sauce
1 tablespoon fish sauce
1 tablespoon sweet chili sauce
2 teaspoons sesame oil
3 green onions, finely chopped
2 teaspoons grated fresh
  ginger
1 tablespoon lime juice
1 teaspoon brown sugar

➤ PLACE FISH in large, shallow non-metal dish.

1 Fill fish cavity with cilantro.

2 Combine garlic, soy, fish sauce, chili sauce, oil, green onions, ginger, lime juice and sugar; mix well. Pour marinade over fish. Cover and refrigerate several hours. Prepare and heat the barbecue 1 hour before cooking.

3 Cook fish on hot, lightly greased griddddle for about 15 minutes, taking care not to burn skin of fish. (Move fish away from the flame and dampen the fire if fish begins to stick to plate.) Brush fish frequently with marinade until flesh flakes easily with a fork, and has turned opaque. Serve with egg noodles and barbecued citrus wedges, if desired.

COOK'S FILE

Storage time: Marinate fish for no more than 2–3 hours.

1

2

3

DILLED FISH WITH LEMON BUTTER SAUCE

Preparation time: 10 minutes
+ 3 hours marinating
Total cooking time: 10 minutes
Serves 4

4 boneless white, firm fleshed
  fish fillets (perch or whiting)
2 tablespoons lemon pepper
1–2 tablespoons chopped fresh
  dill
1/3 cup lemon juice

Lemon Butter Sauce
2 tablespoons lemon juice
1/2 cup heavy cream
3 tablespoons butter, chopped
2 tablespoons chopped fresh
  chives

➤ RINSE FISH under cold water.
1 Sprinkle lemon pepper all over fillets and place in shallow non-metal dish. Combine dill and lemon juice. Pour over fish, cover and refrigerate several hours. Prepare and heat the barbecue 1 hour before cooking.
2 Cook fish on hot, lightly greased barbecue griddle for 2–3 minutes each side or until flesh flakes easily with a fork. Serve with Lemon Butter Sauce, barbecued citrus slices and a green salad, if desired.
3 To make Lemon Butter Sauce: Simmer lemon juice in a small pan until reduced by half. Add cream; stir until mixed through. Whisk in butter a little at a time until all the butter has melted; stir in chives.

COOK'S FILE

Storage time: The fish and sauce are best cooked just before serving.

SWEET AND SOUR FISH KABOBS

Preparation time: 20 minutes
 + 3 hours marinating
Total cooking time: 10 minutes
Makes 12 skewers

1¹/2 lb boneless firm fleshed fish
 fillets
8 oz can pineapple tidbits
1 large red pepper
1 tablespoon soy sauce
2 tablespoons brown sugar
2 tablespoons white vinegar
2 tablespoons tomato sauce
salt, to taste

➤ SOAK WOODEN SKEWERS in water for several hours.

1 Cut fish into 1 inch cubes. Drain pineapple, reserving 2 tablespoons liquid. Cut pepper into 1 inch pieces. Thread pepper, fish and pineapple alternately onto skewers.

2 Place kabobs in shallow non-metal dish. Combine soy sauce, reserved pineapple juice, sugar, vinegar, tomato sauce and salt in small bowl; mix well. Pour marinade over kebabs. Cover; refrigerate several hours. Prepare and heat barbecue 1 hour before cooking.

3 Barbecue kabobs on a hot, lightly greased griddle, brushing frequently with marinade, 2–3 minutes each side or until just cooked through. Serve immediately with cooked noodles and a dressed green salad, if desired.

COOK'S FILE

Storage time: Kabobs are best cooked just before serving. Do not marinate longer than 3 hours.
Variation: Any vegetable can be substituted for pepper; try zucchini, cherry tomatoes, mushrooms or onion.

1

2

3

70

BARBECUED LOBSTER TAILS WITH AVOCADO SAUCE

Preparation time: 15 minutes
  + 3 hours marinating
Total cooking time: 10 minutes
Serves 4

¼ cup dry white wine
1 tablespoon honey
1 teaspoon sambal oelek or
   fresh chopped green chilies
1 clove garlic, crushed
1 tablespoon olive oil
4 (12 oz) fresh lobster
   tails

Avocado Sauce
1 medium ripe avocado, mashed
1 tablespoon lemon juice
2 tablespoons sour cream
1 small tomato, finely chopped
salt and pepper, to taste

➤ COMBINE WINE, honey, sambal oelek, garlic and oil; mix well.
1 Use a sharp knife or kitchen scissors to cut along the soft shell on the underside of the lobster. Gently pull shell apart and ease raw flesh out with fingers.
2 Place lobster in shallow non-metal dish. Pour in marinade; stir well. Cover, refrigerate several hours or overnight. Prepare and light barbecue

1 hour before cooking. Cook lobster tails on hot, lightly greased barbecue grill or griddle 5–10 minutes, turning frequently. Brush with marinade until cooked through. Slice into medallions and serve with Avocado Sauce and a green salad, if desired.
3 To make Avocado Sauce: Combine the mashed avocado, lemon juice and sour cream in bowl; mix well. Add tomato; season with salt and pepper to taste.

COOK'S FILE

Storage time: Avocado sauce can be made 2–3 hours in advance. Before refrigerating, cover with plastic wrap to prevent from turning brown.

STEAMED FISH AND VEGETABLE BUNDLES

Preparation time: 15 minutes
Total cooking time: 10 minutes
Serves 4

4 firm fleshed fish fillets
2 tablespoons prepared
   horseradish
1 small tomato, finely chopped
1/2 cup canned corn kernels,
   drained
2/3 cup grated cheddar cheese
1 stalk celery, finely chopped
1/2 red pepper, finely chopped
3 green onions, chopped
1 1/2 teaspoons dried mixed
   herbs
salt and pepper, to taste

➤ PREPARE AND HEAT barbecue. Grease 4 large sheets of foil, each double thickness.
1 Place a piece of fish fillet in the center of each piece of foil; spread each with a quarter of the prepared horseradish.
2 Top each fillet with tomato, corn, cheese, celery, red pepper and green onions. Sprinkle with herbs, salt and pepper. Bring foil edges together, enclosing fish in a neat bundle.
3 Cook bundle, fish-side down, on hot barbecue grill or griddle 5–10 minutes, without turning, until fish is cooked through. (Check the fish after 5 minutes; cooked fish flakes easily and flesh will turn opaque.) Serve the fish and vegetable bundles immediately, garnished with diagonally sliced green onions, if desired.

COOK'S FILE

Storage time: Foil parcels can be prepared several hours in advance and stored in refrigerator. Barbecue fish bundles just before serving.
Variation: Try other vegetables in the foil, such as grated carrot and zucchini with finely chopped onion.

1

2

3

BARBECUED TUNA WITH ONIONS

Preparation time: 10 minutes
   + 3 hours marinating
Total cooking time: 10 minutes
Serves 4

4 fresh tuna steaks
4 small onions
1 1/2 cups dry red wine
1/4 cup brown sugar
salt and pepper, to taste

➤ PLACE TUNA in shallow non-metal dish.

1 Cut onions in half; slice finely. Sprinkle over fish. Combine wine, sugar, salt and pepper; mix well.
2 Pour marinade over fish. Cover and refrigerate several hours. Prepare and heat barbecue 1 hour before cooking. Drain fish and onion; reserve marinade.
3 Cook tuna steaks and onions on hot lightly greased barbecue griddle for 8–10 minutes or until lightly browned and just cooked through. Pour marinade over tuna and onions a little at a time during cooking.

COOK'S FILE

Storage time: Barbecue the tuna and onions just before serving. Do not marinate for more than 3 hours.
Notes: Tuna steaks should be handled with care, as they can bruise easily at room temperature. Store them in the refrigerator until you are ready to prepare them and avoid turning or handling the steaks when marinating or cooking. Remove them from the heat as soon as they are cooked and serve immediately.
Hint: Tuna flesh is dark and has a strong flavor. To dilute some of this flavor without affecting the texture of the flesh, soak the steaks overnight in lightly salted water. This may whiten the flesh slightly, but will not affect its cooking time.

1

2

3

Steamed Fish and Vegetable Bundles (top)
Barbecued Tuna with Onions.

VEGETABLES & SALADS

MARINATED GRILLED VEGETABLES

Preparation time: 30 minutes
+ 1 hour marinating
Total cooking time: 5 minutes
Serves 6

3 small slender eggplant
2 small red peppers
3 medium zucchini
6 medium mushrooms

Marinade
1/4 **cup olive oil**
1/4 **cup lemon juice**
1/4 **cup shredded basil leaves**
1 **clove garlic, crushed**

➤ CUT EGGPLANT into diagonal slices. Place on tray in single layer; sprinkle with salt and let stand 15 minutes. Rinse thoroughly and pat dry with paper towels.

1 Trim pepper, removing seeds and membrane; cut into long, wide pieces. Cut zucchini into diagonal slices. Trim each mushroom stalk so that it is level with the cap. Place all vegetables in a large, shallow non-metal dish.

2 To make Marinade: Place oil, juice, basil and garlic in a small screwtop jar. Shake vigorously to com-bine. Pour over vegetables and combine well. Store, covered with plastic wrap, in refrigerator for 1 hour, stirring occa-sionally. Prepare and heat barbecue.

3 Place the marinated vegetables on hot, lightly greased barbecue grill or griddle. Cook each vegetable piece over the hottest part of the fire 2 min-utes each side. Transfer to a serving dish once browned. Brush vegetables frequently with any remaining marinade while cooking.

COOK'S FILE

Storage time: Vegetables can be marinated up to 2 hours before cook-ing. Take vegetables out of refrigera-tor 15 minutes before cooking to allow oil in marinade to soften.
Hint: Marinated Grilled Vegetables can be served warm or cold. Serve any leftover vegetables with thick slices of crusty bread or individual bread rolls. Other herbs, such as parsley, rose-mary or thyme, can be added to the marinade. This marinade can also be used as an all-purpose salad dressing. Make up a little extra marinade at the time of preparation and store in the refrigerator, in a screwtop jar, for up to 2 weeks. Olive oil will solidify in refrigerator, so allow marinade/salad dressing to come to room temperature before using.

BEETS WITH MUSTARD CREAM DRESSING

Preparation time: 10 minutes
Total cooking time: approximately
   1 hour 15 minutes
Serves 6–8

2 slices bacon, finely chopped
1 bunch fresh beets

Mustard Cream Dressing
8 oz sour cream
1 tablespoon prepared
   horseradish
1 tablespoon grainy mustard
1/2 teaspoon dry mustard
   (optional)
salt and pepper, to taste
3–4 fresh chives

➤ COOK BACON in frying pan for 5–10 minutes until crisp. Drain on paper towel and set aside.

1 Trim beets by removing stems and leaves. Place in a pan; cover with cold water. Bring to boil, reduce heat and simmer gently 1 hour or until beets are tender. (Cooking time will depend on age and size of beets.)

2 Drain beets and set aside until cool enough to handle. Peel and cut into wedges. (Leave any small beets whole.) Arrange in a serving bowl.

3 To make Mustard Cream Dressing: Combine sour cream, horseradish and mustard in bowl; beat until smooth. Add mustard, to taste; season with salt and pepper. Pour dressing over the beets, top with fried bacon and snipped chives.

COOK'S FILE

Storage: Beets can be cooked ahead of time, peeled and stored in the refrigerator until needed.

ROSEMARY SAUTEED POTATOES

Preparation time: 10 minutes
Total cooking time: 25 minutes
Serves 6

4–5 large potatoes (about 3 lb)
1/3 cup olive oil
1 tablespoon chopped fresh
    rosemary
1 clove garlic, crushed
salt and freshly ground black
    pepper, to taste

➤ PEEL POTATOES and cut into 3/4 inch cubes.

1 Rinse the potatoes in cold water, drain well and dry thoroughly on a clean dish towel.

2 Heat oil in large, heavy frying pan. Add the potatoes and cook slowly, shaking pan occasionally, 20 minutes or until tender. Turn potatoes frequently to prevent sticking. Partially cover pan halfway through cooking. The steam will help to cook the potatoes through.

3 Add the rosemary and garlic, with salt and pepper to taste, in the last few minutes of cooking. Increase the heat to crisp the potatoes, if required.

COOK'S FILE

Storage time: Potatoes can be cooked ahead of time and reheated over the barbecue, in a skillet to which a little olive oil has been added.

Note: Potatoes can be cooked on a large barbecue griddle, provided the heat is not too intense. If the potatoes cook too quickly, the surface will burn without cooking through to the center. Parboil cubed potatoes 2–5 minutes before barbecuing, if desired.

1

2

3

MARINATED ONION, CUCUMBER AND CARROT SALAD

Preparation time: 20 minutes + 2 hours
  15 minutes marinating
Total cooking time: None
Serves 8

2 small cucumbers (12 oz)
1 teaspoon salt
1 large onion (12 oz), finely
  sliced
1/4 cup white vinegar
1/2 cup water

2 1/2 teaspoons sugar
2 teaspoons salt
2 large carrots, peeled and cut
  into thin matchsticks (12 oz)
1 teaspoon sugar
1 tablespoon white vinegar

➤ PEEL CUCUMBER and slice in half, lengthwise.

1 Scoop out the cucumber seeds and slice the flesh into thin sticks. Combine with salt in a bowl and let stand for 30 minutes. Combine the onion, vinegar, water, sugar and 1 teaspoon salt in another bowl. Let stand for 1 hour.

2 Combine carrots, remaining salt, sugar and vinegar in a third bowl; let stand 30 minutes. Rinse cucumber well and add to the bowl with the onions. Mix well. Let stand 1 hour.

3 Combine all vegetables in one serving bowl. Let stand for another 15 minutes. Serve as a sweet-tart accompaniment to grilled meat.

C O O K ' S   F I L E

Storage time: Unused marinated vegetables can be kept for several days in a sealed container in the refrigerator. Make sure the vegetables are covered by the marinade.

1

2

3

SCALLOPED POTATO AND TOMATO GRATIN

Preparation time: 15 minutes
Total cooking time: 1 hour 15 minutes
Serves 8

8 medium potatoes (3 lb)
3 tablespoons butter, melted
1 tablespoon chopped fresh
  herbs (such as thyme,
  marjoram, parsley, rosemary
  and oregano)
1/2 teaspoon cracked black
  pepper
1/2 teaspoon salt
1 1/4 cups heavy cream

2 medium ripe tomatoes
1/2 cup fresh bread crumbs
1 cup grated cheddar cheese
1 tablespoon chopped chives

➤ PREHEAT OVEN to moderate 350°F.

1 Peel and thinly slice the potatoes. Brush the inside of a shallow baking or pie plate with butter, and arrange the potatoes in a circle so that they overlap each other.

2 Sprinkle on the herbs, pepper and salt and pour the cream into the center of the dish. Cover dish with foil, bake for 1 hour. (At this point, the potato dish can be removed from oven, allowed to cool, then refrigerated for later.)

Remove from oven and increase oven temperature to moderately hot 425°F.

3 Thinly slice tomatoes. Remove foil and arrange tomatoes over potato. Scatter evenly with combined crumbs and cheese and return to the oven. Bake, uncovered, 15 minutes until top turns golden. Sprinkle with chives. Serve immediately.

C O O K ' S   F I L E

Storage time: Potatoes with herbs and cream can be cooked in advance, then reheated in a microwave or low oven. Add tomatoes and topping and bake just before serving.
Variation: Thinly slice a medium onion; layer alternating with potato.

1

2

3

Marinated Onion, Cucumber and Carrot Salad (top)
Scalloped Potato and Tomato Gratin.

CURLY ENDIVE SALAD WITH CRISP PROSCIUTTO AND GARLIC CROUTONS

Preparation time: 20 minutes
Total cooking time: None
Serves 4–6

1 large bunch curly endive
1/2 bunch red leaf lettuce
2 red onions
4 slices white or
   brown bread
2 large cloves garlic, crushed
3 tablespoons butter, softened
1 oz feta cheese, mashed
4–6 thin slices prosciutto
1 large avocado

Dressing
2 tablespoons olive oil
1/4 cup sugar
1/4 cup spicy tomato sauce
1 tablespoon soy sauce
1/3 cup red wine vinegar

➤ RINSE ENDIVE and red leaf lettuce in cold water. Shake lightly in dish towel to absorb excess water. Tear endive and lettuce into pieces.

1 Peel and slice the onions; separate into rings. Combine the endive, lettuce and onions in salad bowl or wide shallow dish.

2 Toast bread one side only. Mash garlic, butter and feta cheese into a paste, spread over the untoasted side of the bread. Remove crusts; toast buttered side of bread until crisp and golden on the surface. Cut each slice into 1/2 inch cubes to make croutons.

3 Place prosciutto under broiler for a few seconds until crisp. Remove and cut into 2 inch pieces. Set aside. Cut avocado into thin wedges.

4 To make Dressing: Whisk oil, sugar, tomato sauce, soy sauce and vinegar together in small bowl.
Add prosciutto and avocado to the salad and pour over half the dressing. Arrange croutons on top and serve with remaining dressing.

COOK'S FILE

Storage time: Dressing can be prepared 1 day in advance, but salad must be assembled and dressed just before serving.

CHICKPEA SALAD

Preparation time: 20 minutes
Total cooking time: None or 2 hours
  30 minutes (if using dried peas)
Serves 6–8

1³/4 cups (12 oz) dried chickpeas
  or 2 15 oz cans chickpeas
  (garbanzo beans)
3¹/2 quarts water
¹/4 cup olive oil
1 medium red onion
3 medium tomatoes
1 small red pepper
4 green onions
1 cup chopped fresh
  parsley
2–3 tablespoons chopped fresh
  mint leaves

Dressing
2 tablespoons tahini (sesame
  paste)
2 tablespoons fresh
  lemon juice
2 tablespoons water
¹/4 cup olive oil
2 cloves garlic, crushed
¹/2 teaspoon ground cumin
salt and pepper, to taste

➤ IF USING dried chickpeas (garbanzo beans) place in medium pan. Cover with the water and olive oil. Bring to boil, partially cover and cook over medium heat for 2¹/2 hours or until tender. (Chickpeas will cook in about 30 minutes in a pressure cooker.)

1 Pour chickpeas into colander. Rinse thoroughly with cold water and set aside to drain. If using canned chickpeas, drain well, rinse thoroughly and drain again.

2 Peel the onion; slice thinly. Cut tomatoes in half; remove seeds with a spoon. Cut tomato flesh into small pieces. Slice pepper and green onions into long thin strips. Combine onion, tomatoes, pepper and green onions in a bowl. Add the drained chickpeas, parsley and mint.

3 **To make Dressing:** Combine the tahini, lemon juice, water, oil, garlic, cumin, salt and pepper in a screwtop jar and shake vigorously to make a creamy liquid. Pour over the salad; mix until combined.

COOK'S FILE

Storage: Salad can be made several hours before serving. Store, covered, in refrigerator.

ASIAN NOODLE VEGETABLE SALAD

Preparation time: 30 minutes
Total cooking time: 15 minutes
Serves 4–6

6 green onions
1 lb wide rice (or egg) noodles
4 ripe plum tomatoes
1 medium carrot
12 snow peas
1/2 cup canned baby corn, drained
    and halved
5 oz fresh bean sprouts
1/4 cup roasted peanuts

Dressing
2 teaspoons sesame oil
1/4 cup olive oil
1/3 cup rice wine vinegar
1 1/4 teaspoons sugar
salt and cracked black pepper,
    to taste
1 teaspoon finely chopped fresh
    red chili
1–2 tablespoons chopped fresh
    cilantro

➤ TRIM GREEN ONIONS, cut in thin diagonal slices.

1 Cook noodles in large pan of boiling water 3–4 minutes or until just tender. Remove from heat, drain. Rinse under cold water and drain again.

2 Mark a cross on the top of each tomato. Place in boiling water for 1–2 minutes; plunge into cold water; drain. Peel down skin at cross. Cut tomatoes in half, remove seeds. Cut flesh into narrow strips. Peel carrot,

cut into thin matchstick lengths. Trim snow peas, cut into diagonal slices. Plunge bean sprouts into boiling water 1–2 minutes; drain. Combine all vegetables and peanuts in a salad bowl. Add Dressing and mix thoroughly. Chill briefly before serving. Drizzle with soy sauce, if desired. Garnish with fresh cilantro.

3 To make Dressing: Combine the sesame oil, olive oil, vinegar, sugar, salt, pepper, chili and fresh cilantro in a screwtop jar and shake vigorously to combine.

COOK'S FILE

Storage time: Asian Noodle Vegetable Salad is best made just before serving. Dressing will keep in the refrigerator for 1 week; store in a screwtop jar.

1

2

3

BARBECUED CORN ON THE COB WITH TOMATO RELISH

Preparation time: 15 minutes
Total cooking time: 1 hour
Serves 6

Tomato Relish
16 oz can peeled tomatoes
2/3 cup white vinegar
1/2 cup white sugar
1 clove garlic, finely chopped
2 green onions, finely chopped
4 sun-dried tomatoes, finely chopped
1 small fresh red chili, finely chopped
1/2 teaspoon salt

1/2 teaspoon cracked black pepper

6 large ears fresh corn
1–2 tablespoons olive or vegetable oil
1/4 cup butter
salt to taste

➤ PREPARE AND HEAT barbecue.
1 To make Tomato Relish: Coarsely chop tomatoes or process briefly in a food processor bowl. Combine vinegar and sugar in medium pan. Stir over medium heat until sugar dissolves. Bring to boil. Reduce heat and simmer 2 minutes; add tomatoes, garlic, green onions, sun-dried tomatoes and chili. Bring to boil, reduce heat and simmer 35 minutes, stirring frequently.

2 Add the salt and pepper and continue to cook until the relish has thickened. Remove from the heat and allow to cool.
3 Brush the corn with oil and cook on hot, lightly greased barbecue grill 5 minutes, each side, until corn is soft and ears are flecked with brown in places. Using tongs, lift the corn onto a serving platter and moisten each with a square of butter. Sprinkle with salt. Serve at once with Tomato Relish.

COOK'S FILE

Storage time: Corn is best cooked just before serving. Relish will keep several weeks in the refrigerator, stored in an airtight container.
Note: Serve Tomato Relish as a spicy accompaniment to cornbread and cheese, or with barbecued sausages.

BARBECUED MUSHROOMS

Preparation time: 10 minutes
Total cooking time: 5 minutes
Serves 6

6 large mushrooms
3 tablespoons butter, melted
2 cloves garlic, crushed
2 tablespoons finely chopped
   fresh chives
1 tablespoon fresh thyme
   leaves
1/2 cup grated Parmesan cheese

➤ PREPARE AND HEAT barbecue.
1 Carefully peel skin from mushroom caps. Remove stalks. Combine butter and garlic in a small bowl.
2 Brush tops of mushrooms with garlic butter, place top-side down on hot barbecue griddle and cook over the hottest part of the fire 2 minutes or until tops have browned. Turn mushrooms over. Brush upturned bases with garlic butter; cook 2 minutes.
3 Sprinkle bases with combined chives and thyme, then cheese, and cook 3 minutes more, until cheese begins to melt. Serve immediately.

C O O K ' S   F I L E

Storage time: Mushrooms are best cooked just before serving.
Hint: Mushrooms can also be cooked in a heavy frying pan. Lightly grease the pan with butter and cook mushrooms 2–3 minutes either side. Add fresh herbs and cheese, then place pan under preheated broiler until the cheese has melted.
Any type of mushroom can be used in this recipe. Larger types such as flat or field mushrooms will take longer to cook than button or cup mushrooms. Mushrooms should remain firm and chewy after cooking.

CHINESE VEGETABLE STIR-FRY

Preparation time: 20 minutes
Total cooking time: 6 minutes
Serves 4–6

1 medium red pepper
3 oz oyster mushrooms
15 oz can baby corn
1 lb Chinese cabbage
1 tablespoon olive oil
8 oz fresh bean sprouts
5 green onions, cut into
   1 1/4 inch pieces
2 cloves garlic, crushed
1 tablespoon olive oil

2 teaspoons sesame oil
2 tablespoons teriyaki marinade
1/2 teaspoon sugar
sweet chili sauce, to taste

➤ PREPARE AND HEAT barbecue. Cut pepper in half, remove seeds and membrane. Cut into thin strips. Slice mushrooms in half. Cut any large baby corn in half.
1 Cut cabbage into thick slices, then crosswise into squares.
2 Brush barbecue griddle with oil. Stir-fry pepper, mushrooms, corn, cabbage, sprouts, green onions and garlic 4 minutes, tossing and stirring to prevent burning or sticking.
3 Pour over combined olive oil,

sesame oil, teriyaki marinade and sugar, stir thoroughly to coat and cook 1 minute longer. Serve immediately. Drizzle with sweet chilli sauce.

C O O K ' S   F I L E

Storage time: Vegetables must be cooked just before serving.
Note: Teriyaki marinade is available from most supermarkets. Oyster mushrooms and Chinese cabbage are available from some grocers and most Asian food shops. If unavailable, or if preferred, substitute other vegetables such as zucchini, broccoli, cauliflower, green beans, onions or carrots. All ingredients should be about the same size to ensure even cooking.

Barbecued Mushrooms (top)
and Chinese Vegetable Stir-fry.

RED POTATO SALAD

Preparation time: 20 minutes
Total cooking time: 10 minutes
Serves 8

2¼ lb red potatoes
1 medium red onion
3 slices bacon, finely chopped
¾ cup mayonnaise
¾ cup plain yogurt
3 green onions, finely chopped

➤ SCRUB POTATOES thoroughly and cut into 1¼ inch pieces.

1 Cook potatoes in large pan of boiling water 5 minutes or until just tender. Drain and cool completely. Cut onion in half and slice finely. Cook bacon in frying pan for 5 minutes or until well browned and crisp. Drain on paper towel.

2 Place potatoes, bacon and onion in a large mixing bowl. Combine mayonnaise, yogurt and green onions in a small mixing bowl, pour over potato mixture.

3 Fold the mayonnaise mixture through gently, taking care not to break up the potatoes. Transfer potato salad to a large serving bowl and serve at room temperature.

COOK'S FILE

Storage time: Potato salad can be made up to 1 day in advance. Store, covered, in the refrigerator, allowing salad to return to room temperature before serving.

Note: Do not peel the potatoes for this recipe since the red skin provides color and texture in the salad. Potatoes should be well scrubbed and thoroughly dried before use.

Variation: Use whole baby potatoes in this salad. Cook approximately twice as long as potato pieces.

MIXED HERB TABBOULEH

Preparation time: 20 minutes
Total cooking time: None
Serves 8

3/4 cup bulgur wheat
3/4 cup hot water
2 bunches (flat-leaf) parsley
1 bunch chives
1 1/2 cups fresh basil leaves

1/2 cup fresh mint leaves
4 green onions, finely chopped
3 medium tomatoes, chopped
1/3 cup lemon juice
1/4 cup olive oil

➤ COMBINE BULGUR and hot water in medium bowl.

1 Let stand 15 minutes or until all the water has been absorbed.

2 Remove large stalks from parsley; discard. Wash and dry other herbs; chop well with a large, sharp knife or in food processor. (If using food processor, be careful not to over-process.)

3 Place bulgur, parsley, chives, basil, mint, green onions, tomatoes, juice and oil in serving bowl and toss well to combine. Refrigerate until required.

COOK'S FILE

Storage time: Tabbouleh can be made up to 4 hours in advance.
Note: Bulgur is a cracked wheat, available in some supermarkets and health food shops.

TRI-COLOR PASTA SALAD

Preparation time: 20 minutes
Total cooking time: 10 minutes
Serves 6

2 tablespoons olive oil
2 tablespoons white wine
  vinegar
1 small garlic clove, halved
12 oz tri-color pasta spirals
1 tablespoon olive oil
3/4 cup sun-dried tomatoes in oil,
  drained

1/2 cup pitted black olives
3 oz Parmesan cheese
1 cup quartered artichoke
  hearts
1/2 cup shredded fresh basil
  leaves

➤ COMBINE 2 TABLESPOONS olive oil, vinegar and garlic in a small screwtop jar. Shake well to mix and allow to stand 1 hour.

1 Cook pasta in a large pan of boiling water until just tender. Drain and toss with extra olive oil while still hot. Cool completely.

2 Cut sun-dried tomatoes into fine strips and cut olives in half. Cut Parmesan cheese into paper-thin slices.

3 Place pasta, tomatoes, olives, cheese, artichokes and basil in a large serving bowl. Pour dressing over, remove garlic pieces, and toss to combine. Serve immediately.

COOK'S FILE

Storage time: Salad can be assembled up to 4 hours in advance. Refrigerate until required; allow to come to room temperature. Add cheese and basil just before serving.
Hint: Serve this salad with barbecued steak or roast chicken.

WILD AND BROWN RICE SALAD

Preparation time: 10 minutes
Total cooking time: 1 hour
Serves 6–8

1 cup brown rice
1/2 cup wild rice
1 medium red onion
1 small red pepper
2 stalks celery
2 tablespoons chopped
    parsley
1/3 cup chopped pecans

Dressing
1/4 cup orange juice
1/4 cup lemon juice
1 teaspoon finely grated orange
    rind
1 teaspoon finely grated lemon
    rind
1/3 cup olive oil

➤ COOK BROWN RICE in a pan of boiling water 25–30 minutes until just tender. Drain well and cool completely. Boil wild rice 30–40 minutes; drain well and cool.

1 Chop onion and pepper finely. Cut celery into thin slices. Combine in bowl with parsley and cooked brown and wild rice. Place the pecans in a dry frying pan and stir over medium heat 2–3 minutes until lightly toasted. Transfer to plate to cool.

2 To make Dressing: Place juices, rinds and oil in a small screwtop jar; shake well to combine.

3 Pour dressing over salad and fold through. Add pecans and gently mix through. Serve with bread, if desired.

COOK'S FILE

Storage time: Salad can be assembled up to 4 hours in advance.

1

2

3

SNOW PEA SALAD

Preparation time: 10 minutes
Total cooking time: None
Serves 6–8

5 oz snow peas
1 bunch fresh asparagus
2 medium carrots, peeled
15 oz can baby corn, drained
8 oz can bamboo shoots, drained

Dressing
1/4 cup vegetable oil
1 tablespoon sesame oil
1 tablespoon soy sauce

➤ TRIM SNOW PEAS; cut in half.
1 Remove woody ends from asparagus and cut into 2 inch lengths. Cut carrots into matchsticks.
2 Place snow peas and asparagus in a heatproof bowl and cover with boiling water. Let stand 1 minute; drain. Plunge into iced water. Drain and dry thoroughly on paper towels.
3 Combine snow peas, asparagus, carrots, corn and bamboo shoots in serving bowl. Pour on Dressing. Serve with garlic bread, if desired.
To make Dressing: Place oils and sauce in a small screwtop jar; shake well to combine.

COOK'S FILE

Storage time: Salad is best made just before serving.
Note: Sesame oil is a very strongly flavored oil used in many Asian dishes. It should be used sparingly because its flavor tends to dominate. Sesame oil comes in different strengths, and the darker the oil the stronger the flavor. It is available in the Asian food section of the supermarket or Asian food stores. Once opened it should be stored in the refrigerator.

BABY BARBECUED POTATOES

Preparation time: 20 minutes
  + 1 hour standing
Total cooking time: 20 minutes
Serves 6

1½ lb baby new potatoes
2 tablespoons olive oil
2 tablespoons fresh thyme
   leaves
2 teaspoons crushed sea salt

➤ WASH POTATOES thoroughly under cold water. Cut any large potatoes in half so that all potatoes are a uniform size for even cooking.

1 Boil, steam or microwave potatoes until just tender. (Potatoes should remain whole and intact.) Drain and lightly dry with paper towels.

2 Place potatoes in large mixing bowl; add oil and thyme. Toss gently to coat potatoes; let stand 1 hour. Prepare and heat barbecue.

3 Place potatoes on hot, lightly greased barbecue griddle. Cook 15 minutes, turning frequently and brushing with remaining oil and thyme mixture, until golden brown. Place in serving bowl and sprinkle with salt. Garnish with extra thyme sprigs, if desired.

COOK'S FILE

Storage time: Potatoes can be cooked and marinated 2 hours in advance. Barbecue just before serving.
Note: Sea salt is a pure form of salt that comes in large crystals. Kosher or table salt can be substituted.

1

2

3

KETTLE BARBECUE COOKING

ORANGE AND GINGER GLAZED HAM

Preparation time: 25 minutes
Total cooking time: 1 hour 30 minutes
Serves 20

12 lb ham on the bone
1/4 cup orange juice
3/4 cup orange marmalade
1 tablespoon grated ginger
2 teaspoons dry mustard
2 tablespoons brown sugar
whole cloves (about 30)

➤ PREPARE KETTLE barbecue for indirect cooking at moderate heat (normal fire).
1 Remove ham rind by running your thumb around edge of ham, under the rind. Begin pulling from the widest edge. When rind has been removed to within 4 inches of the shank end, cut through the rind around the shank. Using a sharp knife, remove excess fat from ham; discard fat. (Reserve rind for crackling, if desired. Rub rind with salt and barbecue for 40 minutes.)

2 Using a sharp knife score top of ham with deep diagonal cuts. Score diagonally the other way, forming a diamond pattern. Place ham on barbecue; put lid on barbecue and cook 45 minutes.
3 Place juice, marmalade, ginger, mustard and sugar in small pan. Stir over medium heat until combined; set aside to cool. Remove lid from barbecue; carefully press cloves into top of ham (approximately one clove per diamond); brush all over with marmalade mixture. Cover barbecue and cook 45 minutes more. Serve garnished with clove-studded orange slices, if desired. Ham can be served warm or cold.

COOK'S FILE

Storage time: Cover ham with a clean, dry cloth; store in refrigerator up to 1 month. Change the cloth every 2–3 days.
Note: Leftover ham can be sliced and served with fried eggs, or with grilled tomatoes. Cubed ham is delicious in fried rice. The ham bone can be used for stock or as the basis of pea soup.

WHOLE FILLET OF BEEF WITH MUSTARD COATING

Preparation time: 1 hour 5 minutes
+ 15 minutes standing
Total cooking time: 40 minutes
Serves 6–8

4 lb beef tenderloin
1/4 cup brandy

Mustard Coating
1/3 cup wholegrain mustard
1/4 cup heavy cream
3/4 teaspoon black pepper,
    coarsely ground

➤ PREPARE KETTLE barbecue for indirect cooking at moderate heat (normal fire). Trim meat of excess fat and tendons.

1 Tie meat securely with string at regular intervals to retain its shape. Brush beef all over with the brandy; let stand for 1 hour in the refrigerator.

2 To make Mustard Coating: Combine mustard, cream and pepper in small bowl. Spread evenly over top and sides of meat.

3 Place meat on large greased sheet of foil. Grasp corners of foil and pinch securely to form a tray. (This will hold in the juices). Place lid on barbecue and cook for 30–40 minutes for medium-rare meat. Let stand for 10–15 minutes before carving into thick slices. Serve beef warm with barbecued or grilled vegetables.

COOK'S FILE

Storage time: Beef can be marinated in brandy up to 1 day in advance. Store, covered, in refrigerator.
Hint: Reserve cooking juices left in foil to make a gravy; stir in a tablespoon of prepared mustard.

1

2

3

KETTLE CHICKEN

Preparation time: 10 minutes
Total cooking time: 1 hour 30 minutes
Serves 4–6

3¹/₂ lb whole chicken
salt
¹/₂ teaspoon cracked
   peppercorns
1 whole head garlic
small bunch fresh oregano
¹/₄ cup olive oil

➤ PREPARE KETTLE barbecue for indirect cooking at medium heat (normal fire). Place a drip pan underneath top rack. Remove giblets and any large fat deposits from chicken; wipe and pat dry with paper towel. Season chicken cavity with salt and pepper.

1 Using a sharp knife, cut off top of head of garlic. Push the whole head of garlic, unpeeled, into the cavity. Follow with whole bunch of oregano. Close cavity with several toothpicks or a skewer.

2 Rub chicken skin with salt and brush with oil. Place on grill over drip pan. Close lid on barbecue and cook 1 hour, brushing occasionally with olive oil to keep the skin moist. Insert skewer into chicken thigh. If juices run clear chicken is cooked through. Remove chicken from heat and let stand for about 5 minutes before carving.

3 Carefully separate garlic cloves; serve 1 or 2 cloves with each serving of chicken. (The flesh can be squeezed from the clove and eaten with chicken, according to taste.)

COOK'S FILE

Storage time: Chicken is best cooked just before serving. Chicken can be kept warm in barbecue; open top and bottom vents to prevent further cooking.

Hint: Toast slices of French bread and spread with the soft, cooked garlic. Add a drizzle of olive oil and a sprinkle of salt and pepper. Serve with the chicken or toss the garlic into a salad.

1

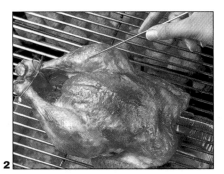
2

3

SPICED SWEET POTATOES

Preparation time: 20 minutes
Total cooking time: 25 minutes
Serves 4–6

1 lb orange sweet potatoes
1/4 cup light brown sugar
3/4 teaspoon pumpkin pie spice

2 tablespoons butter, chopped
1/3 cup orange juice

➤ PREPARE KETTLE barbecue for indirect cooking at moderate heat (normal fire). Peel sweet potatoes and cut into thick slices.

1 Arrange in layers in shallow greased foil pan. Sprinkle over combined sugar and pie spice; dot with butter.

2 Sprinkle over the orange juice.

3 Cover pan with foil, place on top rack of grill, close lid, cook 20 minutes. Remove foil and test with a sharp knife; cook a few more minutes, if necessary. Sprinkle over a little more orange juice if potatoes begin to dry out.

COOK'S FILE

Storage time: This dish is best cooked just before serving.

1

2

3

BARBECUED LAMB SHANKS

Preparation time: 5 minutes
  + overnight marinating
Total cooking time: 45 minutes
Serves 6

2 cloves garlic, halved
1/3 cup olive oil
6 lamb shanks
salt and pepper, to taste

➤ COMBINE GARLIC and oil in small bowl, cover and marinate, at room temperature, overnight.

1 Prepare kettle barbecue for indirect cooking at moderate heat (normal fire). Place a drip pan under top rack. Trim the lamb shanks of excess fat and tendons.

2 Brush the garlic oil generously over the lamb shanks and sprinkle with salt and pepper.

3 Place lamb shanks on the top rack of the barbecue, cover with lid and roast 35–45 minutes or until the meat is tender when pierced with a fork. Serve with barbecued vegetables, such as peppers, and thick slices of chargrilled potato, sprinkled with herbs, if desired.

COOK'S FILE

Storage time: Lamb shanks can be marinated and stored in refrigerator 1 day in advance.

Hint: For a more intense flavor, double the quantity of garlic in the oil and brush over lamb several hours before cooking. Pour remaining garlic oil over shanks before serving.

Variation: Try this recipe with other cuts of meat, such as lamb neck chops, osso bucco, pieces of ox tail and chicken drumsticks.

1

2

3

LEG OF LAMB

Preparation time: 15 minutes
Total cooking time: 1 hour 30 minutes
Serves 6

4 lb leg of lamb
4 cloves garlic
6–8 sprigs rosemary
2 tablespoons olive oil
2 tablespoons freshly ground
    black pepper

➤ PREPARE KETTLE barbecue for indirect cooking at moderate heat (normal fire). Place drip pan on the bottom rack.

1 Trim the meat of excess fat and tendons. Cut narrow, deep slits all over top and sides of meat.

2 Cut the garlic cloves in half lengthwise. Push garlic and rosemary sprigs into slits. Brush lamb all over with oil and sprinkle with black pepper.

3 Place the lamb leg on barbecue grill over drip pan, cover and cook for 1 hour

30 minutes for medium-rare meat. Brush with olive oil occasionally. Let stand in a warm place, covered with foil, 10–15 minutes before carving.

COOK'S FILE

Storage time: Barbecue lamb just before serving.
Variation: Use this same marinade on a 4 lb beef roast or with cut up chicken pieces.
Hint: Barbecue an extra 15–20 minutes if you prefer well-done meat.

BAKED VEGETABLES

Preparation time: 20 minutes
Total cooking time: 1 hour 15 minutes
Serves 6

6 medium potatoes
1/4 cup butter, melted
1/4 teaspoon paprika
1 1/2 lb winter squash
6 small onions
5 oz green beans
5 oz broccoli
2 tablespoons butter,
    chopped

➤ PREPARE KETTLE barbecue for indirect cooking at moderate heat (normal fire). Peel the potatoes and cut in half.

1 Using a small, sharp knife, make deep, fine cuts into potatoes, taking care not to cut all the way through. Take two large sheets of aluminum foil, fold in half and brush liberally with some melted butter. Place potatoes unscored-side down on foil and fold up edges of foil to create a tray. Brush potatoes generously with melted butter and sprinkle with paprika.

2 Cut squash into three wedges, cut each wedge in half. Peel onions and trim bases slightly, so they will sit flat on grill. Brush squash and onions with melted butter. Place tray of potatoes, squash pieces and onions on barbecue grill. Put lid on barbecue; cook 1 hour.

3 Trim ends of beans; cut broccoli into florets. Place on a sheet of foil brushed with melted butter. Dot with

extra butter; enclose completely in foil. Add to vegetables on grill, cook 15 minutes more.

COOK'S FILE

Storage time: Vegetables are best cooked just before serving.
Hint: If barbecuing a chicken or leg of lamb, cook vegetables simultaneously, timing them to be ready with the meat. If vegetables are cooked early, store, wrapped in foil, in a warm place until needed.
Variation: Use any of your favorite vegetables for this recipe. Hard vegetables like turnips and sweet potatoes can be placed directly on grill. Smaller or leafier vegetables, such as mushrooms, spinach or asparagus, can be cooked in foil packets. Cooking times are the same as for a conventional oven.

*Leg of Lamb
with Baked Vegetables.*

SMOKED CHICKEN BREASTS

Preparation time: 5 minutes
Total cooking time: 25 minutes
Serves 4

hickory or mesquite chips
4 boneless chicken breasts, skin removed (2 lb)

1 tablespoon olive oil
seasoned pepper, to taste

➤ PREPARE KETTLE barbecue for indirect cooking at moderate heat (normal fire). Soak wood chips. Trim chicken of excess fat and tendons.
1 Brush chicken with oil and sprinkle over the seasoned pepper.
2 Drain wood chips; spoon about 25 over the coals in each charcoal rail.

3 Cover barbecue and cook chicken 15 minutes. Test with a sharp knife. If juices do not run clear cook another 5–10 minutes until cooked through. Serve at once, with noodles, if desired.

COOK'S FILE

Hint: Soaking the wood chips in wine instead of water for 5 minutes, gives off a pleasant aroma. Use half a cup of liquid to every half cup wood chips.

WHOLE FISH WITH LEMON HERB BUTTER

Preparation time: 15 minutes
Total cooking time: 1 hour
Serves 4

4 lb whole white-fleshed fish

Herb Butter
1/3 cup butter, softened
1 tablespoon chopped parsley
1 tablespoon thyme leaves
1 tablespoon chopped chives
2 teaspoons grated lemon rind

1 small lemon, sliced

➤ PREPARE KETTLE barbecue for indirect cooking at moderate heat (normal fire).
1 Wash and scale fish; pat dry with a paper towel. Place fish on a large sheet of oiled aluminum foil.
2 To make Herb Butter: Blend the butter, herbs and lemon rind in a small bowl and beat until smooth. Spread half of the butter mixture inside the cavity of the fish. Transfer the remaining butter mixture to a serving bowl.
3 Lay lemon slices over the fish, enclose fish in foil and place on barbecue grill. Cover, cook 1 hour or until flesh flakes easily with a fork. Serve with extra Herb Butter.

COOK'S FILE

Storage time: Herb Butter can be made 2 weeks in advance, provided it is well covered and refrigerated. Fish is best cooked just before serving.
Note: Leftover Herb Butter can be spread on hot, fresh bread or served with cooked potatoes and vegetables. It is also delicious served with chicken or steak.

1

2

3

FINISHING TOUCHES

OLIVE SODA BREAD

Preparation time: 20 minutes
Total cooking time: 25 minutes
Serves 8

2 cups all-purpose flour
1 tablespoon baking powder
1 teaspoon salt
2 tablespoons butter, chopped
1/2 cup grated Parmesan cheese
1/2 cup black pitted olives, sliced
1 tablespoon chopped fresh
   rosemary
1/2 cup milk
1/4 cup water
1 tablespoon milk
2 tablespoons grated Parmesan
   cheese

➤ PREHEAT OVEN to moderately
hot 400°F.

1 Brush a baking tray with melted
butter or oil; sprinkle lightly with flour.
Place flour, baking powder and salt
into mixing bowl. Add butter. Using
fingertips, rub butter into flour mixture until it is fine and crumbly.
2 Stir in Parmesan, olives and rosemary;
Add combined milk and water. Mix to
a soft dough with a flat-bladed knife.
3 Turn out onto lightly floured surface, knead briefly until smooth.
Shape into a ball, flatten out to a
3/4 inch thick round.
4 Place dough on prepared baking
sheet. Using a large knife, score dough
deeply into eight portions. Brush with
extra milk and sprinkle with extra
cheese. Bake 25 minutes or until
golden brown and crusty.

COOK'S FILE

Storage time: Soda Bread is delicious
served straight from the oven.

GARLIC FOCACCIA

Preparation time: 20 minutes
+ 50 minutes proving
Total cooking time: 25 minutes
Serves 4–6

1/2 envelope active dry yeast
1 teaspoon sugar
1 teaspoon all-purpose flour
3/4 cup lukewarm water
2 1/2 cups all-purpose flour
1 teaspoon salt
3 cloves garlic, crushed
2 tablespoons olive oil
1 tablespoon cornmeal or
  semolina
1 tablespoon olive oil
2 teaspoons finely crushed sea
  salt

➤ COMBINE YEAST, sugar, flour and water in small mixing bowl.

1 Let stand, covered with plastic wrap, in a warm place for 10 minutes or until foamy.

2 Place extra flour and salt into a large mixing bowl. Add garlic and stir with a knife to combine. Make a well in the center, stir in yeast mixture and olive oil. Using a flat-bladed knife, mix to a firm dough.

3 Turn dough onto lightly floured surface, knead for 10 minutes. Shape dough into a ball, place in a large, lightly oiled mixing bowl. Let stand, covered with plastic wrap, in a warm place 40 minutes or until well risen.

4 Preheat oven to moderately hot 400°F. Sprinkle the base of an 11 x 7 inch baking pan with cornmeal or semolina. Knead dough again for 2 minutes or until smooth. Press dough into pan; prick deep holes with a skewer. Sprinkle lightly with water and place in oven. Bake 10 minutes, sprinkle again with water. Bake 10 minutes more, brush with extra olive oil, sprinkle with sea salt, then bake 5 more minutes. Serve Garlic Focaccia warm or at room temperature, cut into squares.

COOK'S FILE

Storage time: Focaccia is best made on the day of serving.

Variation: Add herbs or olives to the dough, if desired. Use table salt instead of sea salt, if preferred.

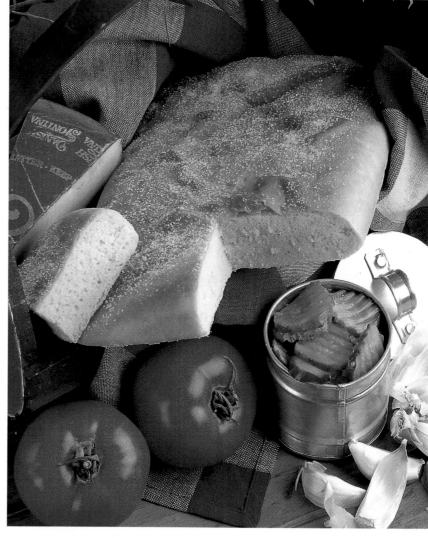

CREAMY LIME TART

Preparation time: 30 minutes
+ 20 minutes refrigeration
Total cooking time: 1 hour 5 minutes
Serves 12

1¼ cups all-purpose flour
½ cup ground almonds
⅓ cup butter, chopped
1–2 tablespoons ice water

Filling
6 egg yolks
½ cup sugar
⅓ cup butter, melted
⅓ cup lime juice
2 teaspoons finely grated lime rind
1 envelope unflavored gelatin
1 tablespoon water
½ cup heavy cream, whipped
½ cup sugar
¼ cup water
rind of 4 limes, finely julienned

➤ PREHEAT OVEN to moderate 350°F.
1 Place flour into a large mixing bowl, add almonds and chopped butter. Using fingertips, rub butter into flour 2 minutes or until mixture is fine and crumbly. Add almost all the water, mix to a firm dough, adding more liquid if necessary. Turn pastry onto a lightly floured surface, press together until smooth. Roll pastry out to fit a 9 inch fluted flan pan. Line pan with pastry, trim edges and refrigerate 20 minutes. Cut a sheet of waxed paper large enough to cover pastry-lined pan. Spread a layer of dried beans or rice evenly over paper. Bake 20 minutes. Remove from oven; discard paper and rice. Return pastry to oven for a further 20 minutes or until lightly golden. Cool completely.
2 To make Filling: Place egg yolks, sugar, butter, lime juice and rind in a medium heatproof bowl. Whisk to combine thoroughly and dissolve sugar. Place bowl over a pan of simmering water and stir constantly 15 minutes until mixture thickens. Remove from heat and cool slightly. Combine gelatin with water in a small bowl. Let stand in hot water; stir until dissolved. Add gelatin mixture to lime curd, stir to combine thoroughly. Cool lime curd to room temperature, stirring occasionally.
3 Fold whipped cream into lime curd; pour into pastry crust. Refrigerate 2–3 hours until set. Let stand 15 minutes at room temperature before serving. Decorate with glazed lime rind. *To prepare glazed lime rind:* Combine extra sugar and water in a small pan. Stir without boiling until sugar has completely dissolved. Bring to boil, add lime rind and simmer 3 minutes. Remove rind from pan, lay on wire rack to drain.

COOK'S FILE

Storage time: Tart can be prepared up to 4 hours in advance.

PAVLOVA

Preparation time: 15 minutes
Total cooking time: 40 minutes
Serves 6–8

6 egg whites
1½ cups sugar
1 cup heavy cream, whipped
4 oz strawberries, hulled and
    halved
2 kiwi fruit, peeled and sliced

1 banana, sliced
pulp of 2 passion fruit

➤ PREHEAT OVEN to slow 300°F. Line a baking sheet with waxed or parchment paper. Mark an 8½ inch circle on paper.
1 Place egg whites in bowl, beat with electric beaters until soft peaks form. Gradually add sugar; beat well after each addition. Beat several minutes until sugar dissolves.
2 Spoon mixture onto baking sheet. Spread over baking sheet, using the circle as a guide. Smooth edge and top with flat-bladed knife.
3 Bake 40 minutes or until pale and crisp. Turn off oven, cool meringue in oven, leaving door ajar. Just before serving, spread with cream and top with strawberries, kiwi fruit, banana and passion fruit pulp.

COOK'S FILE

Storage time: Meringue can be made 1 day in advance and stored in an airtight container. Top with cream and fruit just before serving.

FRUIT KABOBS WITH HONEY CARDAMOM SYRUP

Preparation time: 15 minutes
   + 1 hour marinating
Total cooking time: 5 minutes
Makes 8 kabobs

1/4 small pineapple, peeled
1 peach, peeled
1 banana, peeled
16 strawberries

Honey Cardamom Syrup
2 tablespoons honey
2 tablespoons butter, melted
1/2 teaspoon ground cardamom
1 tablespoon rum or brandy
1 tablespoon brown sugar

➤ CUT PINEAPPLE into eight bite-sized pieces.

1 Cut peach into 8 wedges and slice banana. Thread all fruit alternately on skewers; place in shallow dish.

2 To make Honey Cardamom Syrup: Combine honey, butter, cardamom, rum and sugar in bowl. Pour mixture over kabobs, brush to coat. Cover; stand at room temperature 1 hour. Prepare and heat barbecue.

3 Cook kabobs on hot, lightly greased barbecue griddle 5 minutes. Brush with syrup while cooking. Serve drizzled with remaining syrup. Top with a dollop of fresh cream or yogurt, if desired.

COOK'S FILE

Storage time: Kabobs are best cooked just before serving.

GINGER PEAR CHEESECAKE

Preparation time: 25 minutes
 + 3 hours refrigeration
Total cooking time: 2 minutes
Serves 8

8 oz gingersnap cookies
2 tablespoons sugar
1/2 cup butter, melted

Filling
1/4 cup water
1 envelope unflavored gelatin
12 oz cream cheese
1/3 cup sugar
1 tablespoon lemon juice

1 cup heavy cream, whipped
15 oz can pear halves, drained
 and sliced
2 tablespoons chopped candied
 ginger

➤ BRUSH an 8 inch springform pan with melted butter or oil.

1 Place cookies in food processor bowl and process to form medium crumbs. Transfer to a mixing bowl; add sugar and butter; mix well. Press mixture firmly onto base and sides of prepared pan. Refrigerate 20 minutes.

2 To make Filling: Combine water and gelatin in small bowl. Stand in hot water; stir until dissolved. Cool. Using electric beaters, beat cream cheese until softened. Add sugar and beat 3 minutes. Add lemon juice and beat until combined. Add a little of this mixture to gelatin, mix well. Add gelatin to cheese mixture.

3 Using a metal spoon, fold whipped cream into cheese mixture. Arrange a layer of pear slices on crust; pour over half the cheese mixture. Top with another layer of pears and remaining cheese mixture. Refrigerate 3 hours or until set. Decorate outer edge with chopped candied ginger.

COOK'S FILE

Storage time: Cheesecake may be made up to 8 hours in advance. Store in the refrigerator.
Variation: Use canned peaches instead of pears, if preferred.

CHOCOLATE MOUSSE FLAN

Preparation time: 35 minutes
Total cooking time: 5 minutes
Serves 8–10

6 oz plain chocolate wafer
   cookies, finely crushed
1/3 cup butter, melted

Filling
6 oz semi-sweet chocolate,
   chopped
2 tablespoons heavy cream
2 egg yolks
1 envelope unflavored gelatin
2 tablespoons water
2/3 cup heavy cream, whipped

Topping
1 teaspoon instant coffee
2 teaspoons water
2/3 cup heavy cream
1 tablespoon sugar

unsweetened cocoa powder, for
dusting

➤ BRUSH A 9 inch round fluted flan
pan with melted butter or oil. Line
base with paper.
1 Combine cookie crumbs and butter
in medium bowl; mix well. Press into
base and sides of prepared pan.
Refrigerate until firm.
2 To make Filling: Combine
chocolate and 2 tablespoons cream in
small pan. Stir over low heat until
smooth, stir in egg yolks. Remove from
heat and cool slightly,
3 Sprinkle gelatin over water in small
bowl. Stand in boiling water until
dissolved. Cool slightly and stir into
chocolate mixture. Transfer to
medium mixing bowl. Fold whipped
cream into chocolate mixture; spread
over chocolate crust. Refrigerate until
set. Just before serving, remove from
tin and spread with Topping.
4 To make Topping: Dissolve
coffee in water; combine with cream

and sugar in bowl. Beat until soft peaks
form; spread over mousse. Dust with
sifted cocoa powder just before serving.

COOK'S FILE

Storage time: Mousse flan can be
made up to 1 day in advance. Store,
covered, in the refrigerator.
Variation: If you're not serving the
entire flan at once, spoon topping onto
individual servings and sprinkle with
unsweetened cocoa powder; refrigerate.

MANGO UPSIDE-DOWN CAKE

Preparation time: 25 minutes
Total cooking time: 55 minutes
Makes one 8 inch cake

30 oz can red sliced mango
1/4 cup butter, melted
2 tablespoons brown sugar
1 cup all-purpose flour
1 teaspoon baking powder
1/8 teaspoon salt
1/2 cup ground almonds
3/4 cup butter, extra
1 cup sugar
2 eggs, lightly beaten

➤ PREHEAT OVEN to moderate 350°F. Brush an 8 inch round cake pan with melted butter.
1 Drain the mango slices and reserve 1/2 cup juice. Combine the melted butter and brown sugar, spread over base of pan. Arrange mango slices over sugar mixture.
2 Sift flour, baking powder and salt into large bowl. Add ground almonds; make a well in the center. Combine extra butter, sugar and reserved juice in medium pan. Stir over low heat until sugar dissolves; remove from heat. Add butter mixture to dry ingredients. Stir with a whisk until just combined. Add eggs; mix well.
3 Pour mixture carefully over mango slices. Bake 55 minutes or until a skewer comes out clean when inserted in center. Stand cake in pan 5 minutes before inverting onto wire rack to cool. Serve with whipped cream or ice cream, if desired.

COOK'S FILE

Storage time: Mango Upside-down Cake will keep up to 2 days in an airtight container.

1

2

3

INDEX

USEFUL INFORMATION

All the recipes in this book have been double-tested by our team of home economists to ensure high standards of accuracy. All the cup and spoon measurements used are level. We have used large (2 oz) eggs in all of the recipes. The sizes of cans available vary from manufacturer to manufacturer and between countries—use the can size closest to the one suggested in the recipe.

Glossary of Terms

Devein shrimp: A process to remove the digestive tract down the back after the shell is removed.

Dust: To lightly coat, usually just before serving and often with powdered sugar or cocoa powder.

Florets: The small heads of cauliflower or broccoli that are removed from the main stalk.

Garnish: An edible trimming on the dish to add color and enhance appearance.

Knead: To manipulate dough until it is smooth and elastic.

Peeling tomatoes: To remove the skin from a tomato: mark a small cross on the bottom, then plunge the tomato into boiling water for 1–2 minutes. Then plunge the tomato into cold water. Peel skin down from the cross.

Process: To use either a food processor or a blender to finely chop or puree ingredients.

Simmer: To heat a liquid until small bubbles form and it is on the point of boiling.

Toss: To mix lightly using two wooden spoons.

Until Soft Peaks Form: A method of beating egg whites until light and fluffy and on the removal of the beaters, peaks will form.

Oven Temperatures

Cooking times may vary slightly depending on the type of oven you are using. Before you preheat the oven, we suggest that you refer to the manufacturer's instructions to ensure proper temperature control.

For convection ovens check your appliance manual, but as a general rule, you will need to set the oven temperature a little lower than the temperature indicated in the recipe.

	°F
Very slow	250
Slow	300
Warm	325
Moderate	350
Mod. hot	375
Mod. hot	400
Hot	425
Very hot	450

Cup Conversions

1 cup bread crumbs, dry	= $3^1/3$ oz
fresh	= $2^2/3$ oz
1 cup cheese, grated	
cheddar (firmly packed)	= 4 oz
mozzarella	= $4^3/4$ oz
Parmesan	= $3^1/3$ oz
1 cup all-purpose flour	= 4 oz
wholewheat	= $4^3/4$ oz
1 cup pasta, short (eg. macaroni)	= 5 oz
1 cup semolina	= 4 oz

This 1997 Crescent edition is published by Random House Value Publishing, Inc.,
201 East 50th Street, New York, N.Y. 10022.

Random House
New York·Toronto·London·Sydney·Auckland
http://www.randomhouse.com/

Printed and bound in the United States of America

A CIP catalog record for this book is available from the Library of Congress
ISBN 0-517-18394-3

8 7 6 5 4 3 2 1